WHEN FISH CLIMB TREES

Can-do leadership
in a world of can't

Mel Loizou

mPowr

First Published in Great Britain 2019 by mPowr (Publishing) Limited

www.mpowrpublishing.com

A catalogue record for this book is available from the British Library
ISBN – 978-1-907282-85-0

Cover Design and Illustrations by Martyn Pentecost
mPowr Publishing 'Clumpy™' Logo by e-nimation.com
Clumpy™ and the Clumpy™ Logo are trademarks of mPowr Limited

Engaging, insightful, pragmatic—Mel takes you on a journey to explore who you are, how you work and, more importantly, how you can make positive choices to improve your life both personally and professionally.

What is great about *When Fish Climb Trees* is that it's honest.

Everyone has to manage people, even if they are not a manager. We manage upwards, sideways and every other direction. Nobody is especially good at managing because it's hard and unnatural; the best managers are the ones who know they aren't much good. Most books that try to help navigate the workplace try to tell you what to do, and they all have different silver bullets, none of which work for me because they're not very relevant to me and my circumstances. But *When Fish Climb Trees* is different because it doesn't try to tell me what to do, it tries to help me understand the thing that everyone misses, every day, but when you stop to think about it is blindingly obvious—we're all different...

I loved that *When Fish Climb Trees* is full of real-life examples that made me laugh, because they were eerily familiar to situations I have encountered, and where I have made the same blunders. Next time, I'll try to bear in mind what the book has taught me and maybe I'll manage people a bit better!

When Fish Climb Trees is a very different leadership book. It is a funny, imaginative and heartfelt reflection and a brave challenge to the current state of our workplace, where the majority of people feel undervalued and unappreciated. Mel urges us to consider another way and through wonderful storytelling that is both witty and vulnerable, she offers solutions—backing them up with references to research and more importantly, real life.

Katrina Walding
Head of Business and Customer Services, University of Surrey

This has to be the prettiest, funniest and most practical leadership book that I have ever read and actually enjoyed from start to finish.

The stories that Mel tells are so personal that you hold on to her every word, nod in agreement and chuckle to. This isn't another business expert talking theory at you, it's real work situations supported with real stories and real evidence that can be used to successfully make change...

I am about to lead a big change program at work, which has been really playing on my mind but somehow *When Fish Climb Trees* has given me comfort. I rigorously highlighted key points throughout and completed the 15 downloadable activities and now feel energised and equipped for the journey ahead. This book will firmly have a place on my desk as a go-to reference guide.

Rebecca Paddick
Senior Account Manager, MantisPR

Unlike other books about leadership; often full of dos and don'ts, and step-by-step guides on how to reach your ambitious goals, *When Fish Climb Trees* is about everyday life and "The fundamental skills we need to be better human beings, both at work and at home."

When people buy books on transformative change, they are usually hoping to be shown simple solutions. They want answers to their age-old problems. The integral aspect of this book is that it gently (but firmly) coaxes the reader into discovering the answers they are looking for, for themselves.

Matthew White, Chairman of TUCO (The University Caterers
Organisation) and Director of Campus Commerce, University of Reading

The book isn't your usual management guru homily, this is engaging and empowering. The examples Mel shares are poignant and will be familiar to any reader. The tools you pick up through the *set of scales* really help you to reflect upon your own performance and style and before you know it you are finding ways of making the impossible happen.

This is challenging stuff and has left me with questions which I still need to work through, but with an invigorated clarity and a new personal openness to how I will now approach even the toughest of *cant's* in what I now know is a *can-do* world of leadership.

The mPowr Legacy

Every moment of your life has the potential to be more than every moment of your life. As you invest each day into something greater than yourself—lasting longer than your lifetime, influencing those yet to be born—you create a legacy. A legacy that serves others beyond the minutes, hours and years you will ever spend on Earth. The mPowr Publishing mission is to inspire your legacy—to help you create it through the books and media you develop. Every title we publish is more than the sum of its parts, with deeper impact, broader transformation and, at its heart, a legacy that is yours in this moment, right now.

To Ellie and Louisa

My greatest joy and inspiration

Contents

IT'S **POSSIBLE...**

Doing what you have always done will only ever get you what you have already got. The same results.

According to some, this repeated behaviour can be defined as insanity.

Fortunately, this book is completely sane.

It's not about doing what you have always done. It's about doing things differently. Giving yourself permission to view the world in another way and then, with that shift in perspective, choosing a route that contrasts with the one you would normally take.

If, in the past, you have been attracted by the appeal of quick-fix solutions that repeatedly failed to deliver what they promised, you will be relieved to know this is not the world of *When Fish Climb Trees*.

This cosmos is slightly bizarre and sometimes completely bonkers, but it is also simple and rooted in everyday life. *When Fish Climb Trees* is about long-term sustainable change: transformation and the opportunity to have what we really want.

1

If you are willing to give something new a go, then start by trusting in this wonderful observation, "Every one of us is a genius. But if you judge a fish by its ability to climb a tree, it will live its whole life believing it is stupid."

Enter a world where fish can climb trees and you will see how true these words are. You are a genius. I am a genius. In fact, we live in a world full of geniuses.

Now maybe those superpowers aren't immediately recognisable, but we all have the capacity to be completely and utterly brilliant.

And step one is to stop doing what we have always done.

Mix things up, have a little fun and give something else a go. Like trusting in a world where fish can climb trees.

When most people get to the end of their lives, their biggest sadness is not that they wish they could have worked harder or longer or even that they could have earned more money. It's that they didn't live the life they wanted. They lived within the constraints they themselves (and others) created.

How would it feel if you were to live a life with no regrets?

Embrace the world of *When Fish Climb Trees* and that life becomes a reality.

Change on any level is hard. Perhaps changing our underwear on a daily basis is not difficult. But anything more onerous can be challenging.

What is holding you back from making the sustainable change you desire?

Perhaps you think you know the answer. But the chances are you don't. This book enables you to dig much deeper, into what is really going on for you. What you uncover may surprise you.

2

How many times have you achieved the change you wanted to make?

Often, when we think about the problems we may be having with ourselves, our colleagues, our teams or our business, we believe we know what is causing the angst.

It's the process, the other person, the manager, the organisation. But *never* us.

We very rarely see ourselves as part of the problem or solution. And at work we don't often believe we can make a difference. But WE CAN. Individuals can make a difference.

What difference would you like to make?

Would it be for you personally, or the people around you?

Whatever it is, this book will help you do it. *When Fish Climb Trees* helps you address those elements of your life which are currently holding you back, so you can have the future you want.

Unfortunately, no matter what promises you may have been given in the past, achieving this sort of transformation cannot be hurried. It takes time, grit and determination. However, like most things in life, the results you get will reflect the effort you put in.

At what points in your life have you had your greatest learnings?

Those times when something has just clicked. You finally get what people have been talking about. You have gained another perspective or had a shift in mindset. These learnings may not have happened often but when they do, boy do they make a difference. And once they have occurred, they stay with you no matter what.

Have these moments transpired when you've been at your most focused and serious or when you have been enjoying yourself and having some fun?

For most people it's the latter because let's face it we all like to have a bit of fun. And when we are in that *good* place, without even knowing it, we become more open and flexible. Willing to take on new ideas, thoughts and feelings.

None of us like being told what to do. The chances are if someone tells you what to do, you are likely to do the very opposite. But engage with you, have a conversation and then, yes, you may choose to act differently.

This book does not tell you what to do. It's intended to be enjoyable and entertaining.

It's about everyday life and the fundamental skills we need to be better human beings, both at work and at home.

It's also an exploration into the unique relationship between a business and its people. It provides a route map for individuals who want to find greater fulfilment and live a life without regret and managers who have a desire to become great leaders.

Finally, it considers the responsibility of organisations to create environments which will facilitate this transformation.

Accompanying this book are a set of scales which can be downloaded at...

www.fishclimbtrees.co.uk/register

Please start by adopting one of the key premises of this book. Do *not* do what most people who read books offering transformation do. Don't ignore the exercises or tell yourself you'll come back to them later because that would just be insane.

Download them now. Work through them as you read each chapter. Passively reading about the world of *When Fish Climb Trees*

will not achieve the change you want. You need to engage and give the exercises a go. They will help you get the most from this adventure. Make sure you have them to hand before you read on.

Now that you have your scales, let's venture into the world where fish *can* climb trees.

CHAPTER ONE

THE TOXIC RIVER

Have you ever been angry?

Not just cross but blood-boiling, red-in-the-face furious?

So incensed, you're struggling for breath, your body is shaking, and you feel like you're about to explode?

That's exactly how I was feeling when I returned from leave. At a meeting the previous day, my boss Paul, had behaved in such an appalling way, Anna, a member of my team, ended up in floods of tears, so distraught she had to leave the room.

Anna hadn't done anything wrong, Paul was just in a bad mood, letting his own insecurities come to the fore and wanting to find a scapegoat for his frustrations.

A tough cookie, Anna can handle most people irrespective of their behaviour. That said, she hates being the focus of attention and thanks to Paul's disgusting outburst she had been thrust centre stage in the spectacle he created.

A trusted friend and colleague, Meena, was telling me the story, "You know what Paul's like, that's just how he is. He found Anna afterwards and apologised. He doesn't mean anything by it."

A few years before, I would have been saying those words, making the same excuses. However, in that moment of rage, something shifted in my perspective and I replied, "That doesn't make it ok. Paul behaves in the same abhorrent way over and over again and is always sorry afterwards. That doesn't make it better. If he was truly sorry, he would change his behaviour!"

Something's not right…

You can sense movement, manic and troubled. You're aware of frenetic energy and it's scary. You're frightened and you're not sure what to do.

Day breaks and the sky begins to lighten, slowly turning from the darkest black to an array of beautiful colours, orange, yellow and blue. You look up to the sky, distracted by the beauty of the world around you.

Just for a moment, standing on the bank of the river, you are in awe of this most wonderful sight, breathing in the stillness and pondering these magical moments nature creates every day no matter what madness is going on in the world around you.

A sudden touch causes you to turn your gaze down towards your feet. You spot something thrashing about on the ground. You notice more and more shapes appearing in the sunlight. Wondering what they are, you let your imagination run wild.

Opposite you is a tree. It catches your eye because it looks like a baby tree in comparison to the others, which have been there for many years. In spite of its size *your tree* has space to grow, to develop strong roots and provide a firm foundation on which to continue its journey up towards the sky.

Suddenly you realise what they are. You inhale deeply, not believing what you are seeing because there, on the grass are hundreds of fish.

You are surrounded by them.

They are all shapes and sizes. You notice their different colours, the beauty and intricacy of their scales. Some are big and strong whilst others are miniscule and featherlight as if they will break at any minute.

Tiny droplets of water on some of the scales create an ethereal image. In spite of this, you know the fish are in pain. You look into their eyes which are open wide. You sense their fear and feel them imploring you to help.

Some are writhing around whilst others are motionless but still breathing fast and shallow, as if they are struggling to take their last few breaths of life. For some it is already too late. They are no longer with you, their souls departed to a better place.

You feel their anguish and despair. Your breathing is rapid, and you can feel your heart banging in your chest.

The fish are on the move. You stare in horror, confused. Instead of moving towards the river, the fish are heading for the trees. Some are even trying to climb them. Unbelievably, a few fish have made it onto the lowest branches, which have become their final resting place.

Bewildered, you don't understand what is happening. To survive the fish need to be in water, they need to be in the river. Their natural environment will nurture and protect them.

Why, why, why, you think to yourself, are they being so stupid?

One definition of insanity is *doing the same thing over and over again but expecting different results*.

How many times have you noticed how true this is?

We say to ourselves we want to lose weight, so periodically we put ourselves on a hardcore diet that may deliver quick results but is never sustainable in the long run. Often, we end up heavier than we were before.

Or we want to get fit, so we sign up for the gym, go regularly for at least a week or two and then the gym card starts to gather dust until BANG we decide to repeat the cycle again, prompted by a big event— the overindulgence at Christmas or the need to get *beach ready* for our upcoming holiday.

We have all done this, the question is why?

If someone asked you "Are you insane?" you would probably respond with a resounding "No!" whilst simultaneously thinking "You might be though." However, using the definition of insanity as a basis for our decision the answer is, at least on some level, most of us are just a little bit crazy.

Take my boss Paul. Now he was a great example of someone who was insane, behaving inappropriately to colleagues time and again, but never changing his behaviour. A repeated apology cannot mask the need for a change in behaviour.

Unfortunately, this craziness does not just relate to us as individuals but also the organisations we work for, whether they be big or small, from private, public, or third sector.

How many of us are or have in the past worked for organisations that just seem, a little bit bonkers?

Repeatedly they might receive the same complaints about an aspect of their service. Or the performance of a particular team is consistently below par. Or engagement levels of employees (as tested by the annual staff survey) are poor and yet they continue to behave as they always have.

There might be a *tweak* to the service, the manager of the department may be moved and a team-building day arranged to boost morale, but in my experience, there is very rarely more than a slightly superficial solution applied to the perceived problem. No one wants to

dig deep, turn the issue inside out and upside down to uncover what is really going on.

It's no surprise if this is sounding slightly familiar to you.

There is another wonderful example and if I had an avocado for every time I had seen this pattern play out I would be drowning in guacamole.

I witnessed it numerous times when I was in *paid* employment and subsequently, since being brave and branching out as a *solopreneur* (yes, it is a ridiculous term, but it does make me smile).

What is it?

Staff turnover.

How many times have you seen repeated *staff churn* of a role, a department, or even an organisation? Time and again you see the same roles being advertised and you begin to wonder why.

You have a sense something is wrong, but you just can't put your finger on it.

Back in the day when sustainability was emerging as a subject that needed attention, the University of Studymore created a new role of *Sustainability Officer*. As you can imagine, it was quite hard to recruit *the right person* but eventually a suitable person was found.

They didn't stay long.

Another person was recruited but they soon left and then another and then another. This carried on for a number of years and there was always an excuse: "It's a new job, we were never going to get it right first time / She didn't have the drive / He didn't have the ability to work with others…" and so it went on.

The job description was tweaked, the line manager changed, where the person was located altered, but none of these actions made any difference, no one stayed. The organisation concluded, "We have done everything we can, we can't do any more. It's them not us!"

As a casual observer in this repeated cycle of *advertise, recruit, lose, review, tweak, advertise*, I could offer up several reasons why it was so difficult to find the right person but it is done so with the knowledge that when you are stood on the opposite bank of the river, rather than in the cluster and shaded light of hundreds of trees it is much easier to pinpoint where an organisation is going wrong.

If anyone had asked me what I would suggest (and they didn't) I would have pointed them in the direction of the job description. Firstly, to identify with absolute clarity what they wanted the person to achieve. Secondly, consider the skills and attitude this person would need together with their ability to *fit* the organisation.

Finally, and most importantly, create an environment which would enable this individual to succeed. Do that, and yes, the cycle may have been broken. Instead of which it wasn't, and consequently all that remained was a frustration from an organisational perspective that the right person didn't exist.

During this time there was never any consideration of the people who had come and gone and what impact this habitual cycle might have had on them.

Once we reach adulthood, we spend more time at work than anywhere else. Ask people whether they are truly happy at work and very few people are. So, my question to you is,

"Are you happy at work?"

If the answer is yes, then "Great. Go enjoy yourself!"

If you're hiding under your duvet, vigorously shaking your head, I would ask, "What are you doing about it?" and, "If you're not already

doing something to change your situation, when are you going to take action?"

For those of you who are shrugging your shoulders unsure or would respond with "It's ok, it serves a purpose," I would question, "Is that enough for you? Is a life of shoulder shrugs enough?"

Only you know the answer. Only you can know what is right for you.

When you are in a job that doesn't make your heart sing, it can have a truly toxic impact on every aspect of your life.

A proud southerner, I was born and bred in Pinner, Middlesex (although it no longer exists, Middlesex that is rather than Pinner). All the same, after a few years working in London, I decided to tempt fate, risk a nosebleed and venture north past the Watford Gap. Like many of us, I believed the world which existed twenty miles north of London was scary and bizarre.

At the start, it was an absolute joy to be there. I really enjoyed the change of environment. It's true what they say, the northerners are friendlier than us southerners and it was fantastic to be just an hour's drive from the heart of the Lake District.

However, as the weeks turned into months and I moved into my second year of being told "You've got a right cockney accent," (I haven't, and I took great umbrage at such a suggestion) I began to crave the familiarity of my old life.

Bizarrely I hankered after the hustle and bustle of London and my friends who I had known since school. It was so long ago that the only form of social media was Friday nights down the pub chatting with my mates, a mobile phone would have involved me yanking my home phone out of the wall and stuffing it in my handbag and memos were still the preferred choice of communication at work.

Now, for those of you who don't know what a memo is…

A memo (or *memorandum* to be linguistically correct) was what us oldies used as our primary method of communication long before email.

They were very formal and always began with *Dear*, never *Hi* or *Hey*. We typed our message and finished with *Yours sincerely* or *Yours faithfully*. Using *Regards* (of any sort) was not appropriate.

Once complete, we printed out the memorandum and sent it to the recipient via the internal mail, ensuring the internal envelope (which was different to the *external* envelope) was addressed correctly. Oh, and not to forget, we had to print out a second copy, which was filed away manually. In those days we never felt comfortable just having a digital copy. A paper copy was an absolute must.

What a fantastic example of organisational insanity!

Although it was a bonkers form of communication, memos do offer some valuable learnings we could use in today's digital world.

Due to the lengthy process involved there was no shooting from the hip and firing off a memo in anger or frustration. And we would always consider other more meaningful methods of communication first. Picking up the phone or getting up and speaking face to face with the person who sat two desks down from us.

The final advantage?

There was no copying-in the world and their friend to ensure we had covered our backsides.

Would you really want to copy in ten people if you had to print out ten copies of the memo and address ten separate envelopes?

The train was speeding down the tracks to London. The slight swaying motion, usually such a relaxing sensation was doing nothing to

calm my nerves. The butterflies in my stomach were growing bigger by the minute. I felt sick and my hands were shaking.

Just along the carriage, a young family was sat around a table for four. They were loud and making such a noise it was impossible to ignore them. The young boy was not happy. Sweet wrappers littered the table, along with toys, books and an array of pencils and pens.

There were also rubbers. Lots of different shaped rubbers. A cat, a dog and a lion, a bed, a chair and even a burger.

And chips.

The burger was in a bun with lettuce, tomato and mayonnaise and looked good enough to eat. The chips were the skinny fries variety in a paper cone. They had a smattering of tomato sauce across the top. I hadn't eaten breakfast and it was all I could do to stay in my seat, not rush over and gobble them up.

"I'm sorry Jack but you've had enough sweets. Drink your water." Jack clearly didn't want to. He was crying loudly, his eyes were red, and his nose was running. He was banging his fists on the table and kicking his legs, clearly very annoyed he couldn't have what he wanted.

Normally I would have smiled at such a scene but not on this occasion. Instead I wanted to scream "Shut up, please be quiet! I need to focus."

Have you ever seen a job and thought it was your perfect role?

The only problem is you don't think you have a cat in hell's chance of getting it or even being shortlisted. That was me the day I spotted a job in *The Guardian*. It was my ideal role, based down south, a managerial position, offering a £12,000 pay rise.

In spite of the inner critic in me shouting "You're crazy if you think you're good enough for that job," I decided to apply anyway.

"Well what do you think now?" I asked my inner critic on the morning I received a letter asking me to attend an interview.

"Not a lot," she replied, "they must be desperate or stupid."

At London Kings Cross I waved goodbye to Jack and his family. And the burger. And chips. As I made my way across London on the tube, my inner critic would not stop badgering me. I just wanted her to be quiet and leave me alone,

"If you don't shut up, I'll get the avocado out!"

The silence that ensued was pure bliss.

I finally reached my destination.

My interviewers were two very jovial gentlemen, Ben and Thomas. Ben was a grizzly bear, big and tall with a large beard (it was so big I had to do a quick check to make sure there was nothing growing in it). He had a deep gravelly voice and kind eyes. The sort of eyes that are always smiling no matter what.

Thomas was much shorter. He obviously had bad eyesight as his glasses were thick, round in shape like Biggles' glasses. They caused his eyes to look much bigger than they really were. They also gave the appearance that Thomas was staring at you intently. "He's a bit strange," commented my inner critic.

"Nonsense!"

"Don't surprise him," she warned, "or his eyes might pop out of his head like a jack-in-the-box!"

"SHUT UP!" I replied, trying not to laugh.

Despite all my fears, the interview went well, and I was able to answer all their questions. The butterflies, shaky hands and sick feelings disappeared. It was actually an enjoyable experience.

"Well Melanie, I just have one more question for you. If we were to offer you the job, would you take it?"

"Yes, yes I definitely would. The job sounds just perfect."

Formal interview over, it was now time for the psychometric tests.

"Well you might have been able to fool them in interview, but they're going to find out exactly how crazy you are now," said my inner critic helpfully.

"There's nothing wrong with me, I'm perfectly normal," I replied.

"You are so not! How many people do you think go through the answer paper ensuring the dots they have made are all the same size?"

"Well, you know how I like things to be just so!"

"But that isn't normal. Just wait till they look at your actual answers!"

Having finished the tests, I was sat at a large boardroom table, waiting for Ben and Thomas. My butterflies and shaky hands returned with a vengeance and my inner critic would not stop goading me.

"You do know that they are never going to give you the job. You haven't got the experience, you're just not good enough!"

"PLEASE be quiet!" I begged.

I traced my fingers along the grain of the beautiful oak table. Up and down, slowly, rhythmically. The wood was cool beneath my fingertips and the repetitive motion calming. Eventually the butterflies began to fade, and my hands started to steady. I no longer felt sick and the inner critic finally fell silent.

Suddenly there were muffled voices and the door swung open. Thomas and Ben walked in and sat down.

"So, Melanie how do you think you did?"

Stumbling and stuttering, "Ok I think."

"Well we have interviewed a number of other candidates, but they weren't right. We've just had a quick look at the results of your psychometrics and we think you'd be a good fit with the current team. We'd like to offer you the job!"

Oh my God! Really?

I looked up to find both Ben and Thomas smiling. They were expecting me to say something, but I was in shock and for once the inner critic had nothing to say!

"Gosh, that's amazing, thank you so much!"

"Couldn't you sound a little more professional, a little less gushing?" My inner critic asked. I didn't respond, instead I went into her preferences and ticked the box *communicate by memo only*.

"Sorry," I said. I realised Thomas was speaking with me, but I missed what he was saying because I was too busy, listening to the sound of typing.

"Have you got some time for lunch before you get the train?"

"Yes, yes of course."

We said goodbye to Ben and headed off to the pub around the corner. We ordered food, lasagne and chips for Thomas and a chicken salad for me. Thomas also ordered a bottle of house red.

We chatted over lunch and Thomas told me he lived out in Kent. He was divorced and had two grown up children. Another bottle of wine was ordered, and I regaled Thomas with tales from my northern adventure.

A few hours passed, and it was almost four o'clock. As Thomas saw me into a taxi, I realised I'd had just two small glasses of wine whilst he'd drunk the remainder.

As the black cab slowly made its way through the bustling London traffic, I reflected on the day's events. I should have been ecstatically happy but for some reason I wasn't. My inner critic was frantically typing,

Dear Mel,

Something's wrong, having two bottles of wine with lunch isn't right. That Biggles man would have ordered a third one if you hadn't said you'd had enough.

Perhaps because I was a bit squiffy (two glasses of wine has always been my limit) or far more likely, because I was so desperate to move back down south, I chose not to listen and completely ignored her.

A few weeks later I waved a quick hello to the Watford Gap as I passed it on my journey home, back to my beloved south.

I travelled from Pinner into London on my first day as a fully-fledged manager. I was going to be part of a small team, managing two people within it. "How good is this," I thought to myself as I sat on the tube. Even the inner critic had to agree.

My buoyant mood didn't last. As I opened the door to the office, those good feelings drained away to be replaced by an awful sense of foreboding. All the women who were there, turned towards me and looked me up and down as if I was something the cat had dragged in. "Oh God!"

"You never told me you were going to work in a witches cavern!" laughed my inner critic gleefully.

The day didn't get any better, it was just awful. The chatter carried on around me and if the phone rang and people were deep in conversation, they would just ignore it.

A few days later when Thomas told me in order for the team to get their ISO9002 accreditation for great customer service they had to answer the phone within six rings, I was astounded. He laughed and said, "But if a customer gets an answerphone message that's fine. The regulations don't state the phone has to be answered by a person!"

Walking home from the station on that first day, I cried. The inner critic knew I had made a massive error of judgement but for once she decided to gloat in silence.

It was a living nightmare. It became clear that Thomas was an alcoholic and there were numerous incidents, which involved the flagrant misuse of financial resources. I am also sure some members of the team were taking backhanders.

The whole operation was at odds with my professional integrity. If I was in that situation today, I would speak out. Back then I didn't know what to do, even my inner critic was unsure.

Despite my misery and absolute hatred of the job, I did nothing to change the situation. Sure, I would moan to my family and my friends about everything I was going through (they must have become so bored by me moaning on and on and on) but still I did nothing.

My inner critic knew I needed to act but she encouraged me to remain rooted to the spot. In spite of loathing the job, it somehow seemed easier to stay than go. "You hate it, but at least it's familiar."

"Thank you, inner critic. Have you got anything useful to say?"

"Well you could change company but I'm not sure it would be any different and it could be worse. And you can't just leave without having another job. How would you pay your bills? Right now, you have your cosy flat but do something drastic and you could be homeless within a month."

The inner critic was right and for a while it seemed far easier to stay inert in no man's land. The lethargy remained, and nothing changed.

Nowadays, if I had a client who was in a similar position I might ask "What is preventing you from making a change?" or "How bad do things have to get before you are prompted to take action?"

Back then we (my inner critic and I) didn't have anyone who was willing to challenge our thinking or behaviour. Although, maybe we did, we just chose not to hear them.

Unable to breathe I was flailing around frightened, unsure how to cope with what was happening to me. I became irritable and moody. At home I would fly off the handle for no reason whatsoever.

I felt like a fish out of water. I was one of those fish on the river bank, writhing around in pain, struggling for breath, scared.

The river, which was close by, offered water in abundance.

But that water wasn't good for me. It was lethal. It provided a toxic environment of just going with flow, doing what I had always done. If I chose to jump back in, nothing would change, and I knew eventually the toxicity would fill my gills and destroy me.

Thinking about your own life, what are the *toxic* aspects which are slowly killing you?

Repeated behaviours which are unhelpful, situations that don't make you happy, fear of change.

Maybe you are aware of what these are or perhaps you are just choosing to ignore the signs.

Download the set of scales and complete
The Toxic River *to dig a little deeper.*

23

The venomous river snaking its way around the bank is the reason there are so many fish surrounding you. They have escaped its poisonous flow and made it onto the bank of the river. A knee-jerk reaction, but now they don't know what to do.

They are terrified. The fish need water to survive but if the river can't provide this, what should they do?

Luckily for me, the decision about what I should do, was taken out of my hands because my best friend Karin, saved the day. Picking up the phone, I could hear the excitement in her voice as she said, "Well Ms Loizou, have I found the perfect job for you…"

Change on any level is difficult. Whether we are trying to lose weight, get fit or find a new job, it is very rarely an easy road to travel. Many people would say to get what you want takes determination and resilience. These are necessary prerequisites to meet any challenges that crop up along the way.

Personally, having tried to change various aspects of my life over the years (including losing weight, getting fit and finding a new job as well as a myriad of other changes, some small and some bloody well humungous) I have found, on the occasions when I have been successful, there has been an additional ingredient.

As you might expect, there have been lots of failures along the way but in spite of these or perhaps because of them (they provide the greatest learning opportunities if you choose to take them) I have enjoyed success.

So, what is this magic ingredient?

For me, it's a shift. A shift in my mindset and my thinking. It's not about doing what I have always done, it's about doing something differently. Firstly, though I have to give myself permission.

Permission to be more flexible and allow myself to consider other options. To challenge the way I view the change and possible routes to success. Do this and wow, amazing things start to happen. I gain new perspectives which lead to changes in my behaviour and increase my chance of victory.

So why is it that sometimes I am able to make this shift and sometimes I can't?

Because, at times, I am a little crazy. As human beings we are amazingly complex and screaming at myself, "Move that mindset, Mel!" doesn't work. Goddammit I wish it did.

Johns Hopkins University in the US carried out some research on post-operative coronary care patients and found that 90% of them do not make any change to their lifestyle after surgery.

Many of these patients will have looked death in the eye and know if they don't make changes to the way they live their life, they have a very good chance of going back to that place or somewhere far worse (depending on your views of the after-life and whether there is one). Yet still they choose to make no change.

Now if you don't mind me saying, that is insane. However, given this is the reality, it's easy to see why *changing our mindset* and consequently our behaviour is no easy task.

Take this knowledge to an organisational level and we can now start to understand why 70% of change projects fail. If post-operative coronary care patients will not change their behaviour, what hope do organisations have?

For change to be successful, not only will the organisation need to change but so also will the people within it. Successful change requires a partnership between the individual and the organisation.

Since we now know that inducing heart conditions in all its employees will not provide organisations with the opportunity to create the *shift* that is needed to be the catalyst for change, we have to find something else. Preferably something that will not cause a threat to life but will create the movement of mindset that will increase the odds of success.

For me the answer is simple. Values.

Values are the key to successful change. Understanding an organisation's values and finding ways to connect them to the values of the people who work in the business is the answer to creating sustainable change.

A magical lake. Beautiful with an abundance of clean, free-flowing water.

This is what the fish need and want.

The lake is the polar opposite to the toxic river. Whilst the river will slowly kill the fish, the lake will provide them with an environment where they can thrive, be truly happy and fulfilled. They can have their hearts' desire.

Although they can't yet see the lake, the fish can imagine just what it will be like once they have made the long journey towards it.

What would be in your lake? What would bring you joy and happiness?

Download the set of scales and complete The Magical Lake.

CHAPTER TWO

THE FISHBOWL

You are unique.

You are also beautifully and amazingly complex. We all are. There is not a single person on the planet who is exactly the same as you (even if you are an identical twin there will be nuances between you).

Perhaps if we lived on a desert island with only ourselves and nature for company this fact wouldn't matter. But with over 7.5 billion of us inhabiting planet Earth is it any wonder we can sometimes struggle with the people stuff; understanding ourselves and those around us?

One of my heroes (and completely insightful guy) is Sigmund Freud. The day I was introduced to one of his analogies a light bulb went off in me which was so big it drained my whole street of electricity, the national grid was concerned about what was happening to its energy supply and my electric toothbrush died.

So, what is the analogy that could have such an effect on the nation's electricity supply?

Freud's analogy that our mind is like an iceberg. And it is our mind that drives our behaviour.

Splitting the iceberg into three, Freud uses the levels to denote the different parts of the mind. The first level is the tip of the iceberg which contains our conscious mind. It's sits above the waterline and contains our mental processes. For example, you may be feeling tired, so you decide to lay down and have a rest.

Just below the waterline is the second level which encompasses our preconscious mind. This is a collection of our memories and stored knowledge, almost like a library that we go to when we needed. For example, if I were to ask you where you lived you would be able to answer the question. Without even knowing it you have gone to your preconscious library, found the answer and brought it into your consciousness.

The final level which is the largest and most dense part of the iceberg is our unconscious mind. According to Freud this is the primary source of our behaviour and it is this awareness that provided me with my light-bulb moment.

When we recognise this, we can begin to understand why it is so difficult for us to change what we do. To create a sustainable change in behaviour we first need to create a shift in our unconscious mind.

Wow!

You're in your beautiful lake. There's an abundance of clean, free-flowing water. Swimming near the surface you can feel the warmth of the sun on your scales and as you look ahead you can see shimmering rays of light dancing on the top of the water. It is the most wonderful feeling. You are free and happy. All is good in your world.

Swimming with a big shoal of fish, you can't quite believe you are here. If you could suspend time you would do so right now because your life is just perfect.

You slowly start to move and reawaken from your stupor, realising you are no longer in water. Instead, you are lying on the bank of the river surrounded by your fellow fish. You aren't able to swim freely and there is no sun warming you. You're in pain, struggling to breathe.

Your disappointment is overwhelming when you realise you were just daydreaming. Your current reality is a living nightmare and with so little energy left it is hard for you to know what to do next.

Kate was a coaching client of mine. She was a marketing director for a large PLC who came to me when she was close to burnout.

Constantly exhausted, Kate felt she was no longer making *good* decisions. Irrational and ill-tempered, she was aware her behaviour was starting to alienate her team, her husband, her friends. Kate knew she needed to change something she just wasn't sure what.

At our first coaching session, Kate said "My team are good, but there are just some things I can't trust them to do. I have to do them myself."

It quickly became apparent Kate's lack of trust in her team came, not as a result of their skills or attitude, but her own desire to be perfect. In Kate's world nothing short of perfect was good enough and the only person who could achieve perfection was her.

There are many, many perfectionists out there (I myself can happily claim to be a reformed perfectionist) so I am guessing we all know someone like Kate even if it isn't ourselves!

Over time, Kate began to see whilst she had always worn the perfectionism badge with pride, it was a trait which may not have been as helpful as she originally thought. A breakthrough came the day we worked with her timeline.

The sun was shining, it was a perfect summer's day. The sky was the brightest blue and there wasn't a whisper of a cloud in sight, just a slight breeze to cool the warm air.

It was the school's annual sports day.

Many parents had come along to support their children. They were milling around, chatting, whilst the grandparents amongst them were setting out their deckchairs, deliberating where to put them so they would have the best vantage point.

30

Kate was six years old and in the running race. Stood with her classmates, she searched out her parents. With half an ear on her friends' conversation, Kate was desperately looking around trying to spot them. Today was an important day, her dad had taken time off work specially to come and watch Kate and her sister Alice.

Kate's dad, Dave, was her hero. The youngest of three sisters, Kate shared a special bond with Dave. Whilst her two sisters favoured their mum, Kate adored spending time with Dave, doing all the things he loved: messing about with cars, gardening and watching sport.

Finally, Kate saw her parents and they waved madly to each other. Kate was so happy they were there. She intended to make her dad proud. As a quick runner she was determined to come first in her race.

Kate's race was one of the latter ones and she could feel the tension building. Kate heard Dave shouting for her sister Alice when she took part in the egg and spoon race. His bellows of "Go on Alice. Go on Alice!" were louder than all the other parents and Kate could sense Dave's disappointment when she came last.

"I have to do this" Kate thought to herself, "I want Dad to see me win."

Finally, it was time for the race.

Kate was at the start line. Mary, her best friend, was next to her. Mary was chatting away, but Kate wasn't listening, she was far too nervous. Jumping up and down she was unsure what to do with all the nervous energy building inside her.

Getting hot, beads of sweat were forming on her brow and running down her back. Kate's feet were uncomfortable in her plimsolls. They had grown so much during the year, but her parents kept saying she had to hang on, they would buy her a new pair in September when school began again.

"On your marks, get set, GO!" shouted the teacher. Kate left Mary behind and ran as fast as she could. On her other side was Sarah, who had not long joined the school. Sarah was keeping up with Kate. The faster Kate ran, the faster Sarah ran.

The finish line was coming into sight. Kate was pumping her arms heroically and pushing hard through her legs but, in those final few seconds, Sarah ran past her.

Sarah came first and Kate came second.

Crossing the line Kate burst into tears. She was inconsolable. She'd wanted to win: second place was never an option.

Her dad rushed over and wrapped Kate up in his arms. She sobbed uncontrollably into his belly. He told her how proud he was and said, "Don't worry Kate, you'll come first next year."

This was the precise moment which kick-started Kate's desire to be perfect. Anything less, she believed, was failure.

Have you ever had a similar gut-wrenching experience?

When you are no longer able to think because every part of you is awash with emotion. Time stands still, and you feel like you're having an out-of-body experience. The world shifts, and you know life will never be the same. You are so overwhelmed by feelings of despair you fear they may suffocate you.

These moments happen throughout our life, caused by a variety of events: coming second in a school race, a parent screaming you aren't good enough and you need to try harder, the taunting remarks of the school bullies who made you cry. The day you are told you have a serious illness, the end of a relationship with a partner, the death of a parent.

The list is endless.

And the problem…

What might seem like an innocuous event to you, could have a profound and lasting impact on me and vice versa because we are all different. Without even knowing it, these experiences get stored away in our unconscious mind deep in the part of the iceberg we cannot see. They drive our behaviour and shape the person we become.

As Kate came to the end of her story there was an outpouring of grief for the little girl who hadn't believed coming second was good enough. All Kate had wanted to do was come first and make her dad proud. She was silently sobbing, twisting the hanky she was holding round and round.

Time passed, and the wracking sobs softened until, eventually, they faded away altogether. Kate regained her composure and slowly looked up. Her eyes were red and glassy, she began to smile and there was an imperceptible nod of her head. Kate's signal to me that she was ready to carry on.

Over the next few sessions we worked on reframing Kate's experience. Kate and I explored what this meant for her and identified coping strategies she could use when she felt those perfectionist tendencies creeping back up. I also challenged Kate to let her team have a go at tasks she previously hadn't trusted them with.

It wasn't an easy journey, but Kate slowly began to let go of her long-held belief that *perfection* was the only option. She started being kinder to herself and others.

By delegating more to her team, Kate was able to spend time coaching and developing them rather than doing the work itself. She found this much more rewarding and her team blossomed under this change in her behaviour. Her team, who Kate had once viewed as good, were now classed as great.

By reframing the experience Kate had as a six-year-old girl, she was able to shift her behaviour as a thirty-eight-year-old woman. What an amazing achievement.

Alongside our unconscious mind there is something else that sits in the part of the iceberg that we cannot see.

It's the voice of our inner critic.

You know, the one that usually comes to say hello when we're finding things tough. The one that told me I wasn't good enough to get the job in London.

"Well, ok you did get the job, but it didn't turn out that well for you did it?" reminds my inner critic gleefully.

"You're right, of course. But it was a great learning experience."

"If you say so. So, what's your point?"

"My point is sometimes, I listen to you a bit too much. You hold me back from doing things. There are times when I want to be brave and you stop me with your constant whining, your fear of the unknown and limiting beliefs."

"NO, I don't!" My inner critic shouts. "I just don't want you to fail. Failure is bad. It means you're not good enough. I've seen what failure does to you. You become a little girl again, wanting to curl up in your bed and have a good cry."

"Maybe you're right or maybe sometimes I just need to take a leaf out of Kate's book, and reframe what you are saying."

"Good luck with that one!" taunts my inner critic.

"Well if that doesn't work maybe I should just get the avocado out!"

Silence once again. The avocado. It works every time!

With so little breath and energy left, you know you are going to have to make a decision if you want to survive. You can't return to the river because the toxicity will eventually destroy you, but neither can you stay where you are. To do so would guarantee a quick death.

There's no doubt that escaping the polluted river was the right choice but, in your desperation and haste, you had forgotten to plan for your continued safety. So now it's a question of survival.

What is the bare minimum you need to survive?

A fishbowl. A fishbowl of pure, clean water.

Clean water will revive you. It will nourish your body, soothe your tortured soul and provide you with the breathing space you need to decide what to do next.

You know that the fishbowl is not the ultimate solution, but it will solve the immediate problem. It will also be able to accompany you on the much longer journey that lies ahead.

Download the set of scales and complete The Fishbowl to consider what are the must-haves that need to be in your fishbowl for you to make a start on the journey to your lake.

Dealing with the people stuff is hard and not just because our behaviour is primarily driven by our unconscious mind. There is a myriad of other complications and challenges. The biggest of these is one which very few people are aware of, or, if they are, do little to address.

If at this point you are decidedly shaking your head, begging me not to kill your electric toothbrush as well, I implore you to carry on reading. Have courage, go with it and hear me out.

The other complicating factor is, *people's perception of a situation is their reality*.

What?

Yes, it is a completely bonkers statement. The first time I heard this idea, I smiled sweetly (well it was more of a grimace) at my coach who was imparting her wisdom and thought *Lady, you are completely and utterly crazy.*

Over the years, I have turned this concept over in my mind and looked at numerous examples and although I still sometimes struggle with the idea or more to the point wish it wasn't so, I do believe that it is absolutely 100% true.

Our perception is our reality.

Take the Brexit debate for example. Regardless of your political views, it was a fascinating playground to watch if you were curious about human behaviour. It was also one of the best examples of people standing up for what they believed to be true. Whether you were a *remainer* or a *leaver* you cast your vote based on your version of reality.

The fact is none of us really knows what the future holds. We can surmise and guestimate, but we don't know for sure. When we placed our votes on the twenty-third of June, 2016, it was based on our perception of reality. If we all had the same view, we would never have needed the referendum in the first place.

On a much more light-hearted note, there was also the global debate about the colour of *that* dress. "What colour is the fabric of this dress?" asked one woman on Tumblr. A simple question, it caused worldwide controversy, going viral overnight.

For a while it seemed no matter where you looked people were arguing about the colour of *that* dress. Turn on the radio and people were debating what they saw, switch on the news, the same again and of course it was rife on social media.

Somehow a dress which was actually blue and black was being seen by many as white and gold. In my house there was a 2:1 split. Myself and Louisa, my youngest daughter, saw white and gold, whilst my eldest daughter Ellie, saw blue and black. The debates (well arguments) we had over it you would not believe.

The dress was in fact an optical illusion, but it made no difference to us. What we saw was our perception of reality and no amount of name calling, badgering or shouting was going to shift our point of view. Hilarious!

When have you found yourself in a similar situation?

Totally convinced of your version of reality you stop listening to any view that isn't the same as yours. People with opposing views are seen as difficult and troublesome and no matter what happens you find a way to alter the story in order to reinforce your beliefs. You know you are right, and no one is going to convince you otherwise!

Now that you are in your fishbowl of clean water, you know you are safe, but you want more. You want your dream, the magical lake. Just surviving is no longer enough, it's time to move forward. You know that somewhere out there is a lake holding an abundance of clean water which will enable you to have everything you ever wanted. To be happy and fulfilled.

You're not sure exactly where this place is or how you will get there but you know that you need to make the most of any opportunity that presents itself to you. It's time to be brave. It's time to let go of the experience created by the toxic river and the shackles of the past which have previously held you back.

It's time to embrace the future, opening your heart and mind to the wonderful possibilities still to be discovered on the horizon.

CHAPTER THREE

THE VALUES TREE

Nowadays, we are surrounded by businesses claiming they are values led. The values are on display in their offices and on their websites, but somehow, we just don't trust them. Why?

Perhaps because we have become cynical about words like teamwork, customer service and integrity, popping up so regularly in organisations' values statements. Nearly 30% of Russell Group Universities have excellence as one of their values. Can that really be the case?

Our values should be as unique as our fingerprints.

What are your values? The values which are as intrinsic to you as the colour of your eyes and the size of your big toe?

Find **The Values Tree** *in the set of scales and note down your values on the side of the tree that relates to you.*

Two gorgeous children, a little girl and a little boy are sharing an ice cream. The image is shot in black and white and there's gentle music playing in the background. The voice-over begins, "We are thoughtful... We are thoughtless..."

Sat on the sofa, I was mindlessly flicking through a magazine when this TV advert caught my attention. It captivated me. In just a few moments it showed human behaviour in all its extremes, at its very best and its very worst. The advert took me on an emotional roller coaster and I was intrigued to find out the organisation.

What was the business?

It was a BANK! Yes, a bank and the advert finished with the statement, "We are what we do."

Now I don't know about you, but I couldn't have predicted that. Ordinarily I would have laughed at my own stupidity but not on this occasion. Instead, I could feel myself getting frustrated. I had really connected with the advert, but the final few words felt like a big fat lie.

Never in a million years did I believe this bank could claim, "We are what we do." Well they could, but not in the *good* way it was being promoted.

And herein lies the challenge with organisational values.

So many times, organisations will identify their values through a quick brainstorming exercise, normally involving senior management and occasionally one or two others from across the business. Values identified and sorted. Hand over to marketing to promote.

If this is your experience, either as an individual within a business or as a customer who has had an experience which is polar opposite to the one you expected, given the company's values, then it's no wonder you struggle with the concept values are a fundamental part of individual and organisational success.

It's true I have never worked for or with this particular bank (and the chances are I never will, given what I have just written!) so I can't definitively say their values aren't true. However, as a potential customer I can certainly say "We are what we do," as a statement which encapsulates the bank's four core values does not resonate on any level.

For values to be meaningful they must resonate—for the organisation, the individuals who work there and anyone else they have contact with (suppliers, customers, investors, etc). The values must reflect the behaviours of the people within the organisation. If they don't, the values are worthless, and I would recommend they are ditched immediately.

Remove them from your offices, take them down from your website and forget they ever existed. Superficial values will be doing your organisation more harm than good.

In today's world, we know many businesses and organisations are driven by money and profit. These are their roots and their driving force for growth. No matter what they may claim in relation to their values being core to what they do, they aren't.

For these businesses, values are like sweet cherries hanging from a tree's branches, a *nice to have* alongside customer satisfaction and employee engagement. They can be picked off at any moment and the fruit which replaces them can taste very different, bitter and sour.

And in a storm, the cherries will not protect the trees from the howling wind and the lashing rain. Instead, the slightest gust of air will cause the fruit to fall to the floor battered and bruised, waiting to be trampled overhead.

What are the values of your organisation?

Perhaps they are explicit (written down in a strategy document or used by marketing to promote the business) or maybe they're not so obvious.

If not, think about the repeated behaviours of you and your colleagues. Do these give you a clue as to what the values are? Every organisation will have values even if they haven't been formally identified.

Typically, we think that values are positive but that doesn't always have to be the case. Don't be surprised if you uncover something that would never be used by marketing!

Note down what you uncover on the other side of The Values Tree.

Do your values match with the values of your organisation or are they dramatically different?

Gerry worked for a charity which claimed it was a values-led organisation. With her wonderful Italian and Australian heritage, she was like a roaring open fire in a very serene and tranquil room. A pocket rocket of magnificent passion and laid-back calm all rolled into one.

I met her at a national conference where I had been speaking about the importance of values. We connected through our mutual view of the world. "I have just joined this amazing business which is completely values driven," she said. "It's like a breath of fresh air and I love it."

A few months later, as we were catching up with a walk, through Richmond Park. I was shocked to learn Gerry was looking for a new job. Having been *in* the organisation for a little while it soon became clear the sales pitch of *we are our values* was so not true it was off the scale.

With all the heat of a boiling pan of pasta she said, "Mel, you are not going to believe this. When the results came back from our employee survey that some of the management team weren't living the values, guess what they did?"

"I don't know. What?"

"They changed their values!"

"They what?"

"Yep, they changed their values."

YOU CAN'T CHANGE YOUR VALUES. That's not how it works. Values are not a pair of shoes which can be swapped according to the outfit you are wearing on a particular day.

Neither are values the sweet cherries hanging from the top of the tree.

Values should be the fundamental roots of an organisation, helping it to grow tall and strong. Protecting it during the deadliest storm.

If an organisation really understood their values, they would know they couldn't just alter them on a whim. Or if they did, they would realise they had never really identified their true values in the first place. Values should be as integral to an organisation as its DNA.

There can be a change of leadership, an organisation can change its direction of travel but there should never be a fundamental change to a business' values.

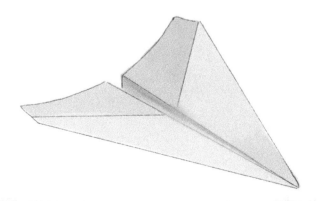

As you look out through your fishbowl, you are pleased to notice that many of your fellow fish have also found their fishbowls. You are not going to be the only fish that survives, you are not going to be alone. It's a comforting thought.

Around the fishbowls there are also countless trees.

The trees are all different. Some have trunks that are smooth and sleek. Others are a wonderful melee of colours and textures. You are drawn to the trees with gnarled trunks and a mishmash of bark. They are warm and appealing, and you sense the wisdom in every one of their knots. The others which are more *polished* look as ominous as the toxic river.

You wonder what the other fish can see. Are they attracted to the same trees or do they prefer the smoother trees?

In the early 1900s, when Freud first used the iceberg analogy, it focused on individuals. For me, it also works really well in terms of helping us understand the collective mindset and behaviour of an organisation.

Imagine for a moment you are an individual working within an organisation. Your mindset and behaviour are an iceberg, as are your colleagues'. When you come together you form one ginormous glacial mass. And the mindset and behaviour of this humungous organisational iceberg is no different to that of the individual.

Therefore, if we want to make any sustainable change, we need to focus our attention below the waterline, to the big chunk we cannot see. The added complication when working with an organisational iceberg is we are simultaneously dealing with lots of mini bergs (the individuals) as well.

When we understand this, we can begin to comprehend why organisations struggle with change and the people stuff.

During my time at the University of Studymore, I spent three years as Deputy Director, with responsibility for many operational teams. Maintenance was part of our department but didn't come under my remit. Consequently, I was really surprised when one day, Robert, the Head of Maintenance, came to find me and said "Mel I need your help…"

How many times have you heard an organisation is bringing in a new system (whether it be finance, HR or Sales) and been told it is going to revolutionise the way they do business?

Tons, no doubt. And how many times have those claims of revolution been realised?

Not very many. Why is this?

Because, whilst improvements in processes, systems and technology can help a business move forward it is the people that make the biggest difference.

How much of the project plans for these new initiatives focused on the people?

Very little. At the start there may have been some initial meetings to understand how people were currently working and usually there was some light touch training at the end but normally that was all. There was never really the time, money or desire to focus on the people. This is why most change projects fail.

There is very rarely an intention to understand how a system or process is used by every individual, day in, day out. If someone raises a concern which doesn't impact the majority it goes on a list entitled *The Difficult Bits We Hope Will Go Away and Be Forgotten*, always with the promise it will be addressed, but never is.

Treat people like this and is it any wonder a new process or system fails? Where is the genuine engagement to gather people's buy-in and comprehend what they need the process or system to do?

The day I received that cry of help from Robert, I was highly intrigued. I had known Robert for a number of years but only as someone who was a distant colleague. I didn't know much about him, although I got the sense he was very passionate about what he did.

Robert and his managers were trying to renegotiate the working hours of the maintenance team. At the time they were working Monday to Friday, 8am-4pm, but this was no longer conducive to meeting the demands of the university.

Robert wanted the team to move to a five out of seven-day rota, with a shift system starting at 7am and finishing at 10pm. They believed this change would enable maintenance to offer a much better, customer focused service. Hearing Robert's plan I wasn't surprised to learn there was resistance.

Negotiations were proving tough, with both HR and the unions involved. Robert wanted my help because negotiations were about to fold and he couldn't let that happen. I could empathise especially when he told me talks had been taking place for three years.

Yes, you read that right, THREE YEARS!

It's no wonder everyone was negotiation weary. Robert and I discussed what had taken place previously and agreed we needed to take a radically different approach if we were to have any chance of success.

In place of a formal meeting room, we opted for an informal space with comfy chairs and coffee tables. Instead of inviting just a few representatives from the maintenance team we encouraged them all to attend.

We replaced PowerPoint, formal minutes and papers with flip charts, brightly coloured pens and Post-it notes (anyone who knows me knows how much I love these tools). Oh, and we had sweets, lots of sweets. No matter what you may think, people adore sweets!

We didn't have a formal agenda, but we did set a very clear intention for the day. Our goal was to leave the room with an agreement for the way forward. Nothing more, nothing less. We wanted the day to be driven by the team who were going to be affected by the proposed changes.

The day of the meeting arrived and we were all nervous. It was make or break and we knew it. Prior to the team arriving you could feel the energy in the room. Rather than being calm and soothing it was erratic and jumpy as though there were thousands of frogs bouncing up and down. Despite our best intentions, we could not relax.

The day didn't run smoothly. It was a roller coaster of emotions. There was clearly anger and mistrust but also a weariness and a sense of

resignation. The one glimmer of hope was the team had not expected to be given the opportunity to voice how they were feeling.

Previously representatives had been speaking on their behalf. But on this occasion the entire team had a voice. And everyone was listened to. As part of the *management team* we didn't always like what we heard. And the team didn't like some of our responses, but at least we engaged in honest conversation.

Chatting with others who had been part of the previous negotiations, they believed this was the first time there had been a frank and open discussion about the proposed changes. The first time the dialogue wasn't littered with management speak and was genuinely two-way.

It was a thoroughly exhausting day for everyone involved but at the end we did achieve our goal. We had agreement we could move forward with the proposals as long as there was a firm commitment to review the working hours once they were up and running.

Robert was ecstatic and we caught up a couple of days later. He was so pleased with the outcome and had been reflecting on the process. He said, "You know what Mel, if only we had done things differently when we started to get stuck, we would have saved ourselves so much time and heartache!"

You see it's true, doing the same things over and over again and expecting different results really *is* insane.

Looking back, it is easy to see the project team (Robert, his senior managers and HR) had focused solely on the process and not the people. In their determination to get the job done, they had chosen not to dwell on the feelings of the maintenance team.

Entrenched in their belief the working hours needed to change, the project team had failed to consider what they understood to be obstructive and defensive behaviour may have driven by fear of change, of the unknown.

One situation, two perceptions of reality.

Despite what we may think, we do not make decisions logically but emotionally. When I learnt this, I was finally able to understand why it is I never choose fruit over a piece of cake even though I know logically fruit is much better for me. And how can this knowledge help organisations?

If you want people to make a change you need to engage with their hearts and minds. On some level, many organisations are getting this right in terms of building relationships with their customers but with their employees, definitely not.

Our TVs and radios are full of adverts trying to connect with us emotionally, just like the bank that claimed *We are what we do*. No longer are companies promoting the features and benefits of their product or service they are trying to make a psychological connection which means we will buy from them.

Why is it businesses can understand the need to connect with the hearts and minds of their customers but not their employees?

Perhaps because the connection between organisations and their customers is far more transactional and straightforward than the one they have with their employees. The relationship between an organisation and its employees is hugely complicated.

It's time to move.

You are very grateful to the fishbowl. It provided you with the clean water and nourishment you needed to rebuild your strength. It has also given you space to think about what is really important to you, what is core to who you are.

Having this time has been invaluable. You know you are ready to begin the journey to your magical lake. Armed with a much greater understanding of who you are you are confident you will make better choices now and only embrace opportunities that fit with your values.

It's time to move into the trees. But the question is which tree will suit you best?

CHAPTER FOUR

BOWL MOVEMENTS

The red velvet curtain rose. Fast and frenetic, the sound of violins, tubas and the French horn filled the theatre.

"I hate you, I hate you, I hate you!" sang a young girl as she ran on stage. There was a thunderous look on her face.

"No, no, no you don't," sang out an older woman as she too, entered the stage. She looked sad and raw emotion came through in her voice.

"You don't understand anything. Nothing, nothing, nothing," warbled the girl, gathering up the ruffles of her long emerald green dress. Stomping up the stairs singing "I hate my life, I hate you, you think you understand, but you don't. I hate you!"

The music and the singing picked up pace, "I want you to leave me alone, life's not fair and you don't understand. You certainly don't." And with a loud clash of the cymbals the young girl threw herself onto the bed. "Life is sooooo notttt fairrrr."

Downstairs, the older lady was singing, "I do understand, I really, really do. I love you, I do. I love you more than you couuuuuuld knoooooow."

The singing stopped but the music continued, the young girl laying on her bed looking mutinous, the older lady tidying the kitchen, looking tired and worn down.

The frenzied music started to slow and soften. The harp and marimba took the place of the violins, tubas and French horn. Slowly, having exhausted so much energy, the young girl sat up and haltingly made her way downstairs, singing softly "I'm sorry, I don't know what came over me, I'm sorry."

As she reached the bottom step, she sang out more loudly to the lady "I am so sorry, I'm really, really sorry. I don't know what came over me." Her voice was tinged with sorrow and regret

"I'm sorry too," sang the lady.

They ran to each other and embraced. Together they sang a beautiful and haunting aria, ending with the words, "I love you, I love you, I love you."

The stage went dark to the sound of rapturous applause.

I blinked, realising I was no longer on the stage of a dramatic Italian opera but at home in my kitchen. The voice belonged not to an operatic diva with dark eyes and a thunderous look but my gorgeous daughter Louisa, who had recently become somewhat of a stranger to me.

I knew deep inside there was still the delightful baby I used to lovingly cradle in my arms. But whilst Louisa was on this journey from child to adulthood, that particular version of her was often lost, replaced instead by a diva monster I no longer recognised.

Perhaps, you have had experience of dealing with this alien species or are able to recall your own antics as you moved through these challenging years, but with Louisa life was extra exciting.

Why?

Since the moment she was born we have all known Louisa was destined for a life on stage. She loves being the centre of attention, she will never miss an opportunity to entertain and she doesn't have a quiet button. It is either loud, louder or loudest. Every member of our household has noise-cancelling headphones.

Louisa is also one of the most empathetic people I know. And I have always been in awe of her understanding of people and their emotions (this is not a proud mummy moment but a statement of fact). She always had an understanding of people which was light years beyond her age and if everyone on the planet had her comprehension, the world would be a better place.

Like all of us she is amazing and complex. Unsurprisingly, to balance out the empathic, outgoing, charming personality, she also has a devilish side. A devil that takes the form of being a complete and utter drama queen. A devil who believes she is the star of the melodrama that is her life and therefore has to act out every emotion to the extreme.

Consequently, during those teenage years I was often subjected to screaming, flouncing off and door banging when I asked a simple question such as, "Louisa, please can you bring your dirty plate over here?"

All around you there is chaos. You see some of your fellow fish are on the move, trying to reach the trees. Some of the fishbowls are bouncing along the ground, whilst others are on their side, the fish once again flailing on the banks of the river.

You understand they want to get to the trees, but you wonder why they are taking this approach which is haphazard and dangerous. A riot is breaking out as the fish try to climb on top of each other's fishbowls to reach their destination.

Fish are launching themselves from their bowls. Some are landing just a few feet along from their fishbowl, whilst others are hitting the trees but only to meet with the full force of their trunks. You watch this happen and squirm as one of your fellow fish falls to the floor never to get back up again.

It's complete pandemonium.

We may not all be as theatrical as Louisa, but we love a good drama, don't we?

Whether it's in the form of the latest novel we are reading, we are watching it play out on a reality TV programme or we are listening to our friends as they have a good old moan about their partner, their family their friends.

We all love drama and the place where we see it play out the most?

At work.

At any one moment there may be numerous dramas playing out—between individuals, between departments, between the senior management team and the rest of the organisation. The dramas are constant and whether or not we are willing to admit it, we love them.

How many hours do we waste on work dramas? Creating them, being part of them and finally discussing the ramifications?

For a moment, consider the dramas you get involved in at work.

What character do you prefer to play? The operatic diva, the nasty villain, the helpless princess, the dashing hero or someone else?

And when you are caught up in these productions, what important information are you missing in relation to your job, your colleagues, the issue at hand?

In the set of scales complete your own **Bouncing Bowls.**

The year 2000, the new millennium, represented a time for fresh beginnings and exciting adventure. For me, I did not choose to jack in my job and travel the world, nor did I reinvent myself as a nomad happy to live in the natural world, having given away all my possessions. Instead I chose something far more thrilling.

I opted to remain rooted to the spot and let reality TV enter my soul. And it all began with the UK premier of *Big Brother*.

The show followed a number of *housemates* who were isolated from the outside world in a custom-built house for a long period of time. The public voted each week to evict one of the housemates until just one remained. The *winner* then received a cash prize.

Why do we love these programmes? Because we get to witness other people's dramas first-hand—the laughter, the tears and the arguments. Let's not forget the arguments because they are the highlight for many people. Watching one play out in front of us is thoroughly bewitching.

And we believe what we are seeing on TV is 100% true. We choose to forget about the rigorous editing that has taken place to ensure the *baddie* looks really bad and the *victim* helpless and without blame.

Real life or a very good illusion? You decide.

When the first couple of series of Big Brother aired it felt like the housemates were a random collection of people like you and I. But as time went on you could sense the show was deliberately recruiting people who would be at odds with each other.

The drama became more elaborate, the arguments bigger and more vociferous until one day I had enough. I hit the red button on my remote control. Big Brother disappeared forever from my life. And my soul.

Numerous other iterations of reality TV began to fill our screens. One of the most popular was *I'm a Celebrity, Get me Out of Here!*

A number of celebrities were taken into the Australian jungle and asked to survive without many of the basics we take for granted in everyday life. For three weeks there were no plumbed-in toilets, power showers or washing machines.

The one *communal* bedroom was situated al fresco, beds came in the form of sleeping bags and there was no privacy from fellow campers. During the day the bedroom became the campers' lounge, dining room and kitchen.

Many of the celebrities adjusted to these changes without too much complaint. However, there was one alteration that many struggled with. The camp food. Just like me at London's King's Cross, the campers had to wave goodbye to burgers. And chips. And any other foodie delight they might love. Instead they were asked to survive on a diet which consisted of miniscule portions of beans and rice.

How would your behaviour change if you were constantly hungry and deprived of some of the most basic facilities we expect in our daily lives?

When I am *starving* (a symptom which can easily develop if I am just an hour or two late for a meal), I know I can succumb to operatic diva moments: as Louisa would happily tell you had she been given the right to reply to her story.

"I can also testify to your utter *divaness*," pipes in my inner critic helpfully.

"Thank you, my friend, but now is not the time for you to speak."

Whilst they were on this adventure, the additional highlight for the campers was the bush tucker trials, which enabled them to win *better* meals for camp. The challenges weren't easy, designed to test the celebrities' mental and physical agility.

Covered in creepy crawlies, enclosed in dark and menacing spaces or encouraged to eat a variety of bugs and parts of certain animals' anatomy (testicles, brains and eyeballs were particular favourites), these trials often had the poor celebrities retching before they had even begun.

With such drama playing out, is it any wonder we became completely addicted to these programmes?

The day I hit the red button not only signified the end of Big Brother but all other reality TV series. I managed to ban them from my life until November 2016.

As soon as my daughters were old enough, they jumped on the reality TV bandwagon. They were hooked the moment they started watching *I'm a Celeb*.

"Mum, it's great, please come and watch it," would implore Ellie.

"It's so funny when they are covered in bugs," chipped in Louisa. Ok, so maybe not the most empathetic comment, but everyone has a down day!

The answer was always no. As a parent I had plenty of excuses up my sleeve; the washing up, the clearing away, the ironing (yeah right, the ironing, as if) but one day I finally gave in and succumbed to their constant nagging.

And the strangest thing happened….

I was riveted. Completely and utterly spellbound. Not by the rows, the arguments or the shouting but by the camaraderie, the supportive environment and the mutual respect the campers had for each other.

It was the polar opposite of what usually happens on reality TV shows and it was the first time in the show's fourteen-year history this had happened. It was completely captivating. And it wasn't just the viewers who were impacted by the change in behaviour, so were the contestants.

The number of meals won in the bush tucker trials went through the roof, meaning meals of rice and beans became the exception not the rule.

Instead of creating a playground where we could witness human behaviour at its very worst, these celebrities created an environment which was positive and encouraging. It set them up for success not failure.

A simple TV programme showing what could happen if people were placed in a climate which was supportive and encouraging rather than one which was full of drama and hysterics.

What would happen if we took this learning and applied it to the places where we worked?

As you watch the drama playing out in front of you, you know there has to be a better way. Rather than your fellow fish randomly launching themselves at trees or trying to climb over each other to get the leverage they need, you should all just take a moment and think.

Consider whether this high-flying tragedy is getting in the way of clear thinking and effective action. Are there other options which will generate greater success? And although you are separated by your individual fishbowls, what would happen if you stopped working in isolation and started working together?

In summer 2012, a sense of national pride gripped the nation. London was hosting the Olympic and Paralympic Games and although there was lots of controversy along the way, not least about the amount of money it was costing the UK taxpayer, no one could deny how this sporting event united the nation.

It was a time of celebration, hope and immense energy.

But not for me. For me, it represented one of the most challenging times of my life.

Nine years previously, there had been great excitement when the university I was working for, confirmed their commitment to being part of the bid for London 2012. The university asked me to project manage

their involvement and I could not have been prouder. I accepted without hesitation.

Life is funny. Sometimes it is impossible to comprehend how a choice we make at one moment in time can cause such mayhem years later.

As part of the negotiations we discussed the need for the relationship with LOCOG (London Organising Committee of the Olympic Games) to be a collaborative partnership.

We agreed they could have access to a large part of the campus for a six-month period during 2012 and for the duration of the Games themselves they could have exclusive use. All the while we would carry on life as normal with our 10,000 students and 2,000 staff.

At first, it seemed like the Games were a lifetime away but suddenly as we hit the final eighteen months, it felt like we moved from a sedate steam train journey on a lazy Sunday afternoon to a TGV train, travelling at 200 miles an hour.

Previously we had been able to enjoy the views as we chugged along the tracks. Appreciating the fields which were a multitude of different coloured greens and admiring the nurturing relationship between the sheep and their newborn lambs, as they stood close together.

With the switch in trains, there was no longer any time to take in the joy around us. The view became a confusing blur.

We were being carried along by the force of the train. What had been a delightful journey became something dark and sinister. Of course, the shift in speed came as no surprise—we had been expecting it. What we hadn't anticipated was the impact this would have on our relationship with the LOCOG team.

Like all of us my boss Paul was an interesting character and he loved being part of a good drama. The incident when he caused Anna to end up in tears was just one of many I witnessed in the years we worked together.

Paul nearly always cast himself in the role of a villain, always looking to argue with other people, constantly overreacting and never afraid to assert his authority over those who worked for him. He was like the pantomime character we all love to hate.

But he also had many other facets to his personality. Paul could truly inspire others.

On the occasions when we got our entire team together, he could galvanise people and rouse their emotions like no one I have ever seen. Often, he would do this completely off the cuff and it was an amazing experience to be part of.

In one-to-one meetings if he decided to share his vision for the future, you could leave the room thoroughly motivated, believing you could achieve anything you set your mind to.

He could also be soft and warm.

Like the time he took me on a long walk round campus when I was distraught about my break up with a partner and he gave me the most comforting bear hug ever. Or the moment he was told a colleague had been diagnosed with terminal cancer and I saw his eyes well up with tears as he tried to hold it together.

Paul had a good soul and he was also beautifully flawed just like you and me.

The challenge was his preference was always to play the devil. So few people saw the softer, kinder side of him and, in the end, Paul alienated himself from those around him.

As Maleficent, his team and colleagues were fearful of him. Whenever he walked into a room, the atmosphere became cold and

ominous. Dressed all in black, evil looking with long talons which could be used to pick his nose or scratch your eyes out, depending on his mood.

Heads down, people avoided his sinister stare, hoping they would not become the focus of his displeasure or wrath.

Occasionally, when someone had enough of his villainous and domineering behaviour, they would deliberately bate him into some display of wickedness. Bravery did not cause them to do this but rather, desperation to escape the grim and dismal environment he created.

And all the time, whilst these productions were playing out, people were paying attention to Paul's antics rather than the real work of the day. On numerous occasions I left a meeting listening to people discussing his behaviour not the true issues we had come together to discuss.

Despite its size London 2012 was a one-off event so people only boarded the fast-moving TGV train when needed. As it was hurtling down the tracks to its final destination, more people got on board and what had been a collaborative and enjoyable relationship became one which was much more transactional.

Unsurprisingly LOCOG's demands increased but instead of wanting to discuss what may or may not have been feasible from our perspective, the conversation shifted to "We want this, you will provide it."

As the lead contact for the university, I had to respond to this change in behaviour. Consequently, with the collective *we* language replaced with *you* and *us* I had to alter my communication. To their very clear "We want," I had to respond with equal clarity and say "Unfortunately, you are not going to be able to have that."

It was a very uncomfortable feeling, but I knew my primary obligation was to look after the university, its students and staff. From LOCOG's perspective they wanted to deliver the best Games ever and at times people completely disregarded the implications of what they were asking for.

It was my job to stand firm and protect the university. Whether I wanted to or not I had to take the university perspective.

Driving through campus after the long Easter weekend in 2012, I was distraught. The six-foot fence we agreed LOCOG could put up to protect the area of the campus which would become *theirs* from the start of June had been erected.

I felt violated. Like someone had broken into my home and stolen a piece of jewellery that wasn't worth very much but meant the world to me. Having such a strong negative reaction did nothing to help me manage the changing dynamic of the relationship with LOCOG, it only made matters worse.

Maybe I didn't feel like I was back in the toxic river, but I did notice my fishbowl becoming unsteady. The precious clean water began sloshing around and spilling over the sides. I was scared I might fall out and once again find myself of the bank of the river. I was expending unnecessary energy and I became weary from playing a role I wasn't comfortable with.

Why was I feeling like this?

In order to protect the university, I was behaving in a way that was at odds with my personal values. Building long-term relationships with people, which are built on mutual trust and respect is core to who I am. As the Games got closer, so the relationship moved further away from being one that worked for me.

Understanding our personal values is key to helping us make good decisions and choose relationships which will be beneficial to us. Values are like our personal compass. When we are living in alignment with them the compass dial is still, and we know we are heading in the right direction.

However, when we are behaving in a way which is at odds with our values the dial becomes confused, continually moving, so we have no idea which way is north or south. We feel lost and out of kilter.

When have you been in a similar situation, working in an environment that didn't align with your values?

How did you feel?

In most working relationships there is usually some give and take because ultimately, we have to continue working with each other. There is always a motivation to find a workable solution, which will usually involve compromise on both sides.

With LOCOG the relationship was completely different. The team would deliver the Games and disappear from our lives never to be seen again. Given these circumstances it was very difficult to build a *normal* business relationship. Relations became purely transactional and as the person who often had to say no, I hated it.

For several months the drama with LOCOG dominated mine and my team's working life. It was incredibly difficult for us to handle this whilst simultaneously focusing on our day-to-day business. September is one of the busiest months in the academic calendar as students return from their summer vacation.

It was tough dealing with the conflicting priorities but somehow through grit, determination and fantastic team work we made it through. The Games came to an end, our students returned to campus and slowly life returned to normal.

My fishbowl started to steady as once again the water became calm.

It was only when I was reliving the experience with the wise woman who was my coach, I was able to unpick why this drama was so much more destructive to me than others I had previously experienced. Never before had I been in a situation which was so at odds with my values.

Leaving the coaching session, I finally understood why our values are so important to us and if we want success, happiness, fulfilment, then we need to live a life aligned to them.

My core values are family, love, honesty, building quality relationships and nurturing others.

For a moment, I'd invite you to think about something you are proud of. Something that when you think about it you can't help but sit up a little taller. It might make you smile, it might make you feel like all is good in your world.

Now be curious as to why you are so proud. Don't force your thoughts. Sit with it a little while. Enjoy the voyage of discovery.

The answer may not come to you for a few moments, several days or even longer but when it does you will have the key to unlock a deep understanding of your values and what's really, truly important to you.

In your set of scales find **Your Soul Values** *and note down what you discover.*

How does this fit with what you identified on The Values Tree?

Are the values the same or different?

Hurrah! You have the solution. You know how you can work together to ensure the drama stops and more of your fellow fish make it into the trees.

A s-ling-shot. A s-ling-shot will solve your problems. Working together you can launch your fellow fish into the trees, ensuring they do not hit the trunk but land safely in the branches.

What a fantastic idea. You have a way forward and you are sure it

is going to work.

CHAPTER FIVE

THE S-LING-SHOT

What question in an employee survey typically receives the lowest marks?

Working environment? No.

Pay? No.

Feeling appreciated for the work you do? Yes.

What a sad indictment of the work environments we create for ourselves.

Not everyone will agree. For some people getting paid for doing a job is sufficient reward. They do not feel the need to be appreciated for the work they do, and they can't understand why other people get so hung up on the need to feel valued.

People go to work to get paid. Saying thank you and demonstrating gratitude is just fluffy mumbo jumbo that isn't necessary.

The reverse is true. Being recognised for who we are and what we do contributes to our self-esteem and when this is lacking it can have a truly devasting impact on ourselves and the wider community.

Knife crime in the UK is on the increase and we have some of the worst fatal stabbing rates in the world. For many young people, who have never been shown any appreciation in their lives, becoming part of a gang is the only way they can start to feel they belong. That they can validate their existence as a human being.

Of course, there are many reasons why our young people are joining gangs, but a lack of acknowledgement is a contributing factor to the choices they make.

Can you imagine possessing so little self-worth, having barely been shown any love or compassion, you join a gang to fill these voids in your life. And once you have been accepted into this world, you do whatever is asked of you without thought or feeling.

To hurt, maim or even kill other human beings. Your desolation is so great you are no longer able to decipher between right and wrong. The lives of other people pale in comparison to your need to be accepted and recognised for who you are.

If you still believe showing appreciation is unnecessary *fluff*, then I would urge you to think again.

And it's not just in the gang culture we see the impact of our behaviour playing out. Many years ago, my colleagues and I were devastated by the news that a fellow workmate had died. It hit us hard because this man was a husband and father to two young girls. He had everything to live for.

Sadly, he took his own life. We will never know the reasons why, but as his work colleagues we were asked by his family not to attend the funeral.

No matter what some people tell themselves we all want to be appreciated at some level. Whether it's for the work we do, the contribution we make to our community or just for being the person we are. Appreciating someone can take just a few seconds but have an impact which is far greater than you can ever imagine.

As a child my parents drummed into me the need be considerate of others and have good manners. Apparently sticking chips up my nose

and pretending to be a walrus was not appropriate behaviour at the dinner table and neither was trying to eat my hamburger rubbers.

I was also told it was important to say thank you whenever I was given something and show kindness wherever possible. I adopted the same approach with my children.

"Don't forget to say thank you," I would remind Ellie when her godmother would give her sweets. "Remember to ring Grandma to say thank you for your birthday present," I would encourage Louisa.

"Well that's all well and good but how about you show me some appreciation every once in a while?" grumbled my inner critic.

"I am not sure you deserve it" I replied.

"Of course, I do. Look at everything I do for you."

"Mmm, I'm not so sure about that."

Many of us are brought up the same way. A gentle reminder here, a word of encouragement there. These basic principles are hammered home until they become unconscious habits. By the time we reach our teens, we automatically say thank you to someone who opens the door for us, when a cashier gives us change, and when a car stops to let us cross the road.

And on the odd occasion when someone doesn't say thank you, we get annoyed and think "how rude!"

Saying thanks is basic manners. So, why is it the most basic of human behaviour can go out the window when we are at work?

Perhaps it's because we are too busy paying attention to the dramas which are playing out in front of us. Or we believe to improve performance at work we need to focus on what's wrong rather than what is working well. As a result, we forget to celebrate success and say thank you for a job well done.

A group of you pull back. On the count of three, one, two, three, you let go of the s-ling-shot and your fellow fish flies through the air, targeting the tree. You hold your breath, and everything slows down as you watch what happens. The fish lands safely in the tree and there is a massive uproar. Success! Your idea has worked.

The fish are clambering over each other, wanting to be the next one in the s-ling-shot. Once again you pull back and on a count of three let go. This time there are no cries of jubilation. The fish lands just short of the tree.

Silence now as the fish stop vying for your attention. Tentatively, one brave fish moves forward volunteering to go next. On the count of three the s-ling-shot is released, and the fish goes flying in the air. This time instead of falling short the fish continues to fly high above the tops of the tree and lands on the far side.

Despite this failure other brave fish choose to try their luck.

One of my clients was a department at the University of Wellread. They wanted to use the university's values to underpin a change management programme which would deliver a one team approach and improved customer service.

When we began working together, the university's values had already been identified. In keeping with 30% of Russell Group universities, one of their values was excellence. The others were integrity, respect, collaboration and ambition.

They were a large team, so I worked with a small group of people from across the different sections to really dig deep and understand what these words meant to them and how they related to their personal values.

If you were asked to describe excellence, what would you say?

Quality. High standards. Being at the top of your game.

The day I asked this question to my group, these were the responses I was expecting. When the team fed back their thoughts, I wanted to jump ten foot in the air, sound the party whistles and do a celebratory dance that would embarrass my kids for the rest of their lives.

Unfortunately, as their facilitator I could do none of these things. Well I could but they would have asked security to escort me off campus and I didn't want that. Instead I opted to tell them how bloody amazing they were and how I could never have anticipated what they came up with.

The value excellence meant:

- Creating good morale. Feeling valued and being recognised for the work you do. They believed this would lead to
    - A positive attitude, *which would lead to*
        - Quality work (using themselves as a benchmark. Most of us are much harsher critics about our own work than anyone else)

How completely formidable was their thinking?

In order to deliver excellence at work, we need to create an environment which enables people to be recognised and valued for the work they do. How can we do this?

Well one of the quickest, cheapest and easiest ways is to use those two little words, the words our parents drummed into us as children.

THANK YOU.

Gracias. Tak. Merci. Danke.

Saying thank you. Such a simple thing to do and yet we don't do it enough in the workplace. There is an expectation it should always be managers saying thanks to their team, but why should that be the case? Saying it to your peers is just as powerful and if you ever say it to your manager, well you will be giving them the best gift ever.

Being a manager can be a totally thankless task. So, if you have an awesome manager, or they do something brilliant, I dare you, go say thanks and watch what happens!

Why is it *normal* behaviour becomes so difficult at work?

What would you do if a friend told you they had been given some news which totally rocked their world?

An announcement which left them feeling scared and vulnerable, that called into question their future.

Would you give them a big hug or reach out to touch them in some way? Would you listen to their fears and empathise with the myriad of emotions they were experiencing?

Of course you would.

What you would not do is turn your back on them, shut the door and send an email expressing your sorrow.

Why then do we behave like this at work?

The s-ling-shot. It isn't achieving the results you'd anticipated. It was a brilliant idea that should have increased the number of fish making it safely into the trees. But it hasn't. Ten attempts have resulted in two successful landings, three minor injuries, three serious wounds and two fatalities.

Whilst you were expecting to have some failures along the way you were not anticipating any fatalities. The results are haphazard, and a successful outcome is not guaranteed. You need to review your thinking. There's nothing wrong with the target destination but how you get there needs to be reconsidered.

For most people being told there is a possibility they are going to be made redundant is one of those gut-wrenching moments. When the world stands still and they are so awash with emotion they no longer feel connected to their physical body.

I was twenty-four when it happened to me. Working as a sales manager in a London hotel, I was called into the General Manager's office and told to sit down.

I sat in the green leather chair and looked across the large antique desk directly into the cold blue eyes of Nick, the man who had been my manager for the past nine months. Since joining the team I'd had very little contact with him. He was always very aloof and if he passed me in the corridor, he would look straight through me never acknowledging my existence with even a smile or a polite hello.

Apprehensive, I was looking around the room for something to focus on. There was nothing on the plain cream walls so eventually I dragged my eyes back to Nick's. He quickly looked away, trying to avoid eye contact. Somehow, I just sensed he was going to deliver bad news.

With no preamble, Nick dived straight in and told me he had decided to make some organisational changes and I would be advised at the end of the week whether or not my job had been affected.

There was no softening of the message, or appreciation of what this might mean for me. There was an audible sigh when he finished speaking and then he looked at me directly with his heartless eyes. A subtle movement of his head indicated he was done, the meeting was over, and I needed to leave.

His cold and callous behaviour had a crushing effect. In that moment every bit of confidence I ever had was shattered into millions of tiny pieces. It would take years to repair the damage done in that second. Nick didn't care though. He had done his job, time to move on and find his next victim.

Although my mind knew what I needed to do, my body would not oblige. I was rooted to the chair and I did not have the strength to move even an inch. A few seconds passed and eventually I was able to gather myself up and leave the room.

As my hand grasped the brass door knob, I turned and quietly said, "Thanks for letting me know." My parents would have been proud that even in that moment of desperation I was able to remember my manners.

I left with as much dignity as I could and headed straight for the ladies' loo. Not the most salubrious of places but it was somewhere I could lock the door and be alone to gather my thoughts. I was dazed and shocked. I had not seen it coming.

Of course, I realised the underlying message; I was going to be made redundant. Feeling completely winded, I had no idea what to do. A part of me wanted to walk out of the hotel and never come back but I realised it wasn't the wisest move.

"What did Nick want?" Sammy, my colleague asked when I returned to the office.

"Nothing much, he just wanted to let me know about some changes that may be happening," I replied.

Sammy didn't push it, he could sense something wasn't right. Usually hot on the heels of the slightest hint of gossip, I was surprised when he bent over to go back to the contract he was reading.

My footsteps were slow and heavy when, five days later, I walked out of the hotel for the final time. Weighed down with worry, every step was deliberate and painful. I no longer had a job, but in spite of this, I knew the bills would still keep coming.

A plan of action was required but it was impossible to think clearly. All I wanted to do was get home and shut the world outside. Once inside, I crawled under my duvet and began the slow process to recover from the emotional injuries I had sustained.

When have you been absolutely sideswiped by an unexpected decision or event?

Plundered into despair because you hadn't seen it coming and it completely knocked you off your feet. It left you lying hurt and alone on a cold, dark floor. Wondering if the ants and the other little beasties were getting out their knives and forks, tying napkins around their necks as they prepared to come and feast on your devastation and despair.

Broken and defeated you are unsure you will ever be able to get back up again.

People were laughing and hugging each other. Some had bright eyes, whilst others were smiling wistfully. Janet was hugging Ann tight. Clearly embarrassed, not knowing what to do, Ann decided her only option was to hug Janet back.

When she was finally set free, you knew there would be red marks on Ann's arms. Marks that did not represent pain but total and utter happiness.

More whoops of joy and louder clapping. The atmosphere was electrifying, and whilst I knew I should bring this wonderous moment to a close I didn't want to. Instead I let it come down slowly, drawing to its own natural conclusion.

All the money in the world could not buy the feelings which were in the room at that very moment. What had caused the outburst of such wonderful emotion?

Janet saying thank you to Ann, her line manager.

Often when we have to deliver bad news at work, we choose to forget we are dealing with human beings who have feelings and emotions. Instead we opt to behave in a way that is in complete contrast to how we would treat a friend in need.

Instead of human contact and empathy we choose to focus our attention on the process. After all, a process is much more predictable and safer than a colleague's emotions. We convince ourselves if we follow the process to the letter we will get to the end, unscathed. We will avoid all that unnecessary emotional *stuff* and the outcome will be just as good if not better.

However, there is a major flaw with this thinking. By focusing on the process, we are able to protect ourselves, our feelings and our emotions. What we fail to consider is the collateral damage for those people who are impacted by the process. Whilst we may be safe and secure following the procedure, those around us could be having an emotional breakdown.

Is that right?

Is it good manners?

Is it kind?

Let's consider redundancy. It is one of best examples of organisations hiding behind a process.

The threat of redundancy can be one of the most stressful times in our working life. It is arduous for both the people who are overseeing the redundancy programme and the individuals whose lives may be impacted and yet what do most organisations do?

They follow the process as if they are dealing with inanimate objects and forget about feelings and emotions. At a time when organisations should show the greatest empathy to their employees, they typically show the least.

How would those responsible for the redundancy programme change their approach if it was a member of their family or a close friend whose job was going to be put at risk?

Happily, ensconced in my home office, the familiar ping sounded, telling me I had a new email. Yet another advantage of the old-fashioned memo was they only ever arrived twice a day instead of constantly twenty-four hours a day, seven days a week, 365 days a year!

At the time I was working as an associate for a consultancy firm which was based on a university campus. We all had university email addresses and were on the *All Staff* distribution lists.

I opened the email. It was an announcement to all staff advising them the university was beginning a restructure programme. Over the next three months individuals would be advised if their jobs were at risk.

There were no kind words offering support and understanding. It was cold, harsh and to the point. It smacked of someone following a process and forgetting about the poor people who would be reading the message.

My heart sank, and I felt really sad. Of course, the content of the email didn't affect me directly but even so, I was quickly taken back to

being twenty-four years old and sat in Nick's office feeling numb from the news my job was at risk. I empathised with the university staff who at that moment were reading the announcement.

Imagining their pain was not difficult.

Sadness was quickly replaced with anger. Did the senior management team not consider the impact such an email would have? It's true there is no easy way to let people know a reorganisation is imminent, but surely there has to be a better way than a mass email? What a thoroughly awful and cowardly way to treat people.

Janet and Ann had been attending a Values workshop I was delivering as part of University of Wellread's change programme.

The workshop had been designed in conjunction with the small group who had initially dug deep into the values and proved they had formidable ideas.

I loved their bold thinking. It had come through in their understanding of the values. And once again, as we created a workshop for their colleagues, their audacious ideas came to the fore.

As part of the section dedicated to the value of excellence, I read out feedback to each attendee. The comments had come direct from their line manager, explaining what it was they most valued in the individual concerned.

As you can imagine, gathering the feedback for more than three-hundred individuals was no easy task. But the rewards of doing this were far greater than we ever could have imagined.

I felt like I was giving each person a present they had secretly been hoping for but had never dared to believe they would get. Without exception, people's reaction was positive. Some were embarrassed whilst others welled up. Some smiled like the proverbial Cheshire cat, others looked totally shocked at receiving such wonderful praise.

Whilst people's reactions didn't surprise me, I hadn't expected each piece of feedback to result in a round of applause. Just like success breeds success, it seems the same can be said of positivity and encouragement.

And then of course there was the session Janet and Ann attended. Having finished the feedback section, I was ready to move on when Janet suddenly asked me a question.

"Mel, my manager is in the room, can I thank her?"

"Of course," I replied.

The outpouring of emotion I witnessed is something I will never forget. It resulted in what I can only describe as a massive hug fest as other members of Ann's team decided to join Janet in saying thanks and giving her a hug.

Without doubt it is my favourite facilitation moment ever.

Saying thank you, showing our appreciation is so powerful. The power of those two words should never be underestimated and we can all do more of it, at home and most definitely at work.

In your world, who are the people you appreciate the most?

Your partner, your children, your family. Your friends, your colleagues, your next-door neighbour who keeps an eye on the house when you are on holiday.

Why are you thankful to them?

Are they always there for you, whatever you need; do they love you unconditionally; is your life just richer for having them in it?

Do they have any idea what they mean to you?

My challenge to you is to write a list of all those people you appreciate.

**Using The S-ling-shot *in the set of scales,*
*create a scorecard of appreciation for each person.***

*Identify why you appreciate them and the best way for you to say thanks.
Not from your perspective but from theirs. What would have the biggest
impact for them?*

*It might be those two little words, or it might be a handwritten memo,
sorry I meant note. It may even be something as simple as baking their
favourite cake or turning your phone off and being fully present in their
world for just a few moments.*

*The gesture doesn't have to be grand (in fact it probably shouldn't
be) but it does have to come from the heart and be 100% genuine.*

*Decide when you will deliver your thanks. And when you do, notice
what happens. For you and for them. I bet it generates a feeling money can
never buy.*

"Thank you, thank you, thank you," you say to one of your fellow fish. After some real soul searching and blue-sky thinking, one of the fish has come up with another proposal to get you up into the trees.

There are a number of advantages of this idea. Firstly, it involves a much sturdier structure which cannot be sent off course as easily as the s-ling-shot. Secondly, it will also protect the fish and their fishbowls as they are transported from the banks of the river to the branches of the tree.

Finally, and most importantly, it will provide the fish with an opportunity to clarify exactly where they are going, their ultimate destination. The magical lake with its abundance of clean water.

It is a completely awesome idea and if you're really honest, you wish you had thought of it first.

What is this device?

It's an es-scale-lator. A fabulous, wonderful, es-scale-lator, powered by gratitude.

CHAPTER SIX

...I received f...

...earing her say "I ...
pause that ...

...experience ... ...th one of ... ...ssroad moments
ignore her ...
and exper... ...choice to ...
needed to ... ...my kno...
...opportun... ...with every part of my ...
"So b... ...hands
end of my ... ...est adventure ...
could have anticipa... ...planned for.

It was a conundrum involving vast numbers o...
interactions and relationships, complex business functions and the

WFCT

CHAPTER SIX
The ES-SCALE-LATOR

The phone call I received from Karin that day changed my life.

Hearing her say "I have found you the perfect job," I paused. A ... e that was just a tiny bit longer than it ever should have been.

Karin provided me with one of those crossroad moments we all ... ce in the adventure that is our lives. I had a choice to make, ... claim or pursue it. In that quiet pause all my knowledge ... ce came to pass, and I knew with every part of my being I ... b the opportunity with both hands.

... he biggest adventure of my professional life. Near the ... path I was to come across a challenge, which I never ... d or planned for.

... drum involving vast numbers of people, their ... nships, complex business functions and the

CHAPTER SIX

The ES-SCALE-LATOR

The phone call I received from Karin that day changed my life.

Hearing her say "I have found you the perfect job," I paused. A pause that was just a tiny bit longer than it ever should have been.

Karin provided me with one of those crossroad moments we all experience in the adventure that is our lives. I had a choice to make, ignore her claim or pursue it. In that quiet pause all my knowledge and experience came to pass, and I knew with every part of my being I needed to grab the opportunity with both hands.

So began the biggest adventure of my professional life. Near the end of my chosen path I was to come across a challenge, which I never could have anticipated or planned for.

It was a conundrum involving vast numbers of people, their interactions and relationships, complex business functions and the responsibility and accountability for a sum of money most of us can never imagine having unless we won the lottery several times over. I became director of a university department of 600 people, 21 different business functions and a budget of £28 million.

The journey to get there, having only one managerial role behind me, was not an easy one. It was the voyage of a lifetime, made up of lots of little pauses, moments and decisions, all of which brought me unimaginable joy and learning.

When I was given this wonderful challenge, I knew I would need all my accumulated skills and experience and a whole heap of others I didn't even know about, to deliver what was being asked. My task—to improve service levels, increase profitability and create a culture of innovation. Yikes!

Unsurprisingly, as is the case in many organisations, the department was doing ok.

However, having been part of the team for a number of years, I was aware a silent killer was out there, growing and spreading like a cancer throughout the department. It was slowly eroding away the foundations of the team, moving towards the very heart of its existence. If left untreated, it had the potential to do untold damage.

Whilst some individuals were very happy working for the department, there was a large majority who were demotivated. For numerous years restructures had been talked about, so it was no surprise people were fearful of the future and what it might mean for their jobs, their livelihood.

There was also a silo mentality that the casual observer may not have witnessed but, oh my God, did it come to the fore when things went wrong. If ever there was a complaint or failure in service, how quickly did the different service functions baton down the hatches and look to blame other teams.

Finally, and in some ways not surprising given the other two underlying issues, there was a real lack of trust that played out at all levels throughout the department. There was a lack of trust between service functions, a mistrust of management and most importantly a distrust amongst themselves as individuals and all their wonderful potential.

Imagine for a moment you are an assistant football manager who has, for some time been, watching your team from the sidelines. You've been waiting patiently in the wings until the opportunity arises and you are offered the position of manager.

Whilst some may look at the challenge and think you are bonkers to take it on, you have a different perspective. Perhaps, there is a degree of naïve optimism, but you can't wait to implement the changes you believe will make the biggest difference to the performance of your team.

That's how it was for me and just like you as the newly appointed football manager, the question remained, "Would the changes I make really have the impact and effect I imagined?"

Hurrah! The es-scale-lator seems to be working. It is a wonderful improvement on the s-ling-shot. Fish are now being transported safely from the bank of the river into the tree of their choice. There are no casualties or fatalities and those that are able to make it on to the es-scale-lator, seem happy and confident that they are going to make it to their next stop.

Leading any sort of change requires vision. And it starts with absolute clarity about where you want to be at the end of the change period.

Holidays are great, aren't they? They give us the opportunity to step away from routine and spend quality time with our loved ones. And what is one of the first decisions we have to make when we decide we are going to take a break?

Where we are going, the destination.

If we tried to plan a holiday without knowing this, we would get ourselves in a right pickle.

We could book flights to Cyprus, a villa in Tuscany and pack nothing more than flip-flops when what we really need is a hefty pair of walking boots.

It is no different with change programmes. As Stephen Covey says, "You need to start with the end in mind."

It was early January and my partner and I decided we didn't want the festivities of Christmas and New Year to end so we booked ourselves a wonderful mini break.

Bearing in mind it was January in the UK, most people would have opted to go somewhere warm and cheerful: Egypt or the Canary Islands. Not us. Instead we decided a weekend in Brighton would be a wonderful adventure. We booked a hotel on the seafront and paid extra for a room with a sea view.

Arriving late Friday afternoon, lashing wind and rain greeted us. The rain was so heavy it created a mist, which meant when we looked out of our bedroom window all we could see was grey. It felt like the sea had completely disappeared and we were surrounded by a bubble of dull and dreary dishwater.

What a wonderful start to our adventure.

Fortunately, when we woke on the Saturday morning the bubble had burst and the day was dry and bright. Brighton is a wonderful foodie destination, so we decided to venture out and asked reception for recommendations on places that did an awesome breakfast.

Following their directions, we made our way through the cobbled streets of Brighton and turned the final corner. As we did, we couldn't quite believe our eyes.

There was a queue outside the restaurant and our first thought was, "Blimey this must be good."

Unlike most Brits we hate queuing and therefore there were a few moments of "Shall we? Shan't we?" before we finally decided we were on an adventure so why not live dangerously and go for it. We joined the queue.

In front of us was a young family, mum, dad and their ten-year-old son, Toby. Dressed in grey jogging bottoms, a red t-shirt and blue superman hoody, he was jumping up and down, impatient to get inside.

"Dad how long are we going to have to wait?" asked Toby.

"Not long," his dad replied patiently.

"Can I have my usual, pancakes, bacon and maple syrup?" he asked.

We laughed, and Toby turned around.

"Have you been here before?" asked my partner and suddenly the five of us were chatting away like old friends who hadn't see each other for a while.

The family were from London and had often visited the restaurant's other branches. They loved it and were emphatic in their belief we should try the pancakes.

Before we knew it, Toby, his mum and dad had been seated and it was our turn.

The chap managing the door warmly expressed his gratitude to the people who were leaving and thanked, those people like us who had been patiently waiting for a table.

Inside, the restaurant had a fantastic vibe and as we were led up a circular staircase my senses were on fire. The noise from the other customers, the restaurant's decoration, the rickety feel of the wooden

staircase and the beautiful mix of foodie smells created a heady combination.

Somehow, I just knew we were going to have an awesome experience. Upstairs the restaurant was as packed as the ground floor and I was shocked when we were given a booth that could seat six people. Having spent years in hospitality I knew the key to profitability was maximising bums on seats, so it threw me somewhat.

Rob our waiter was from New Zealand. As he took our order, I couldn't fail to notice the tattoos on his arms. They were very unusual, and I suspected each one told a story of a poignant moment in Rob's life. One in particular drew me in: a lake of the brightest blue with snow clad mountains in the background. Rob explained it was a scene from one of his favourite places back home. "Beautiful," I said.

As the fish make the journey on the es-scale-lator they are able to better plan for the future. No longer focused on the ground they are looking out beyond the tree's branches. They still can't see their magical lake, but they sense they are getting closer.

And as they are moving forward, the fish are gaining greater clarity about what they want the lake to offer them when they finally arrive. For some fish just being in the safety of the trees is sufficient. For the moment they do not need or want for anything more.

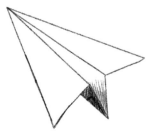

It's a great feeling when you walk into a venue and just love it.

That's how it was for me. Whether it was the service, the physical environment or being surrounded by people of all ages and nationalities having a good time, I had in just a few moments fallen completely, head over heels in love with this place.

Intrigued and wanting to find out more I took out my phone and typed in the name of the restaurant. *The Breakfast Club.*

Interestingly, the feelings I was experiencing sat in The Breakfast Club in Brighton also leapt out from the pages of their website. As I read a little of the club's history, I became really excited. I suddenly got it. I understood why this place was speaking to me.

Without even knowing it, we had stumbled on a business that was truly values led. What a completely unexpected discovery. I made it my mission to find out more.

Becoming director, it would have been easy to assume my vision was built around the remit I had been given, to improve service levels, increase profitability and create a culture of innovation. However, these were merely goals to be achieved.

The vision needed to kill the cancer which was spreading through the department and address the issues of demotivation and lack of trust as well as break down and destroy the silo mentality. The vision had to be big and bold and it absolutely had to deliver results. If not, the department would succumb to its silent killer.

During my fifteen years at the University of Studymore I had a complete blast. I loved what I did, the people I worked with and what we were able to achieve. It was never a chore to get out of bed in the mornings and there were times I had to pinch myself to believe I was really being paid for doing a job I adored.

And that's what I wanted for the people in the department. That was my vision. I wanted to create an environment where people had the same experience as me. They wanted to get up and come to work and, once there, they thoroughly enjoyed what they were doing.

They were completely motivated and felt appreciated for their contribution to the work they did. They came together as one team, knowing they could rely on each other even during the tough times.

It wasn't utopia because of course there would always be days when people didn't want to come in to work. People would still be carrying out tasks they didn't enjoy like filing (although thank goodness the era of the memo had long since passed so there wasn't as much paperwork as there once had been) but it was a world away from the cold and ominous environment they endured under Maleficent's reign.

Achieving this vision, would kill the cancer for good and enable us to meet the goals we had been set.

"For me the hospitality industry is all about taking care of other people. My job is to find people who want to do this. Once I have, then I need to look after them and create an environment which will enable them to thrive."

Sat in the basement of The Breakfast Club in Hoxton, I was chatting with Jonathan Arana-Morton, one of the co-founders of the business. Contacting him via LinkedIn I had never in a million years expected to be invited over for a chat.

Ensconced in the coolest office I had ever been in with fabulous wooden benches, comfy seating areas complete with bright coloured cushions and signage that made you smile, my senses were impacted on every level. However, as Jonathan began to speak the surroundings disappeared into the ether. I became absorbed in what he had to say.

He began by thanking me for making contact. Brighton had been the first venue they had opened outside London and he was unsure whether they would be able to create the same vibe when they weren't able to be there every day. I assured him he had nothing to worry about.

Jonathan was completely humble. He didn't believe what he had achieved with his sister-in-law Ali was anything out of the ordinary. It was just the way he ran his business. He was grateful to his customers who gave up their hard-earned cash to eat at The Breakfast Club but more importantly he was grateful to his team who gave up their time to come and work with him.

And it wasn't just about being good to his people. Jonathan and Ali also wanted to be good to their community. Whilst the business attracts people of all ages, there is definitely a leaning to the younger crowd. In spite of this they work closely with Age UK and a whole host of other charities, many chosen by The Breakfast Club team.

Interestingly it was only in the last few moments we spoke about finances. Jonathan and Ali believe being good at what you do and enjoying it will be enough to ensure the money comes in. That the wages are paid and the mortgage payments met.

This is a business where values are the fundamental roots and force for growth and development. Values focused on looking after the people in the business, so they can look after others, whether they are customers or the wider community.

What an absolutely fantastic business model.

Now it would be easy to think Jonathan had been primed by some PR person to say what he did. But having sat opposite him, looked into his eyes and breathed the same air as him I can tell you the words he spoke came from his heart.

Jonathan and Ali had a vision and it hadn't been created in a boardroom or carefully crafted by a communication expert. It came from the very core of who they were. And as a result of a having such a powerful vision and strong values they were able to create a phenomenal business.

In this instance money and profit were not the roots of the business tree but big juicy cherries hanging from the branches. The cherries on this tree were far bigger and tastier than those on the trees, whose roots were financial.

Having a vision that so clearly comes from the heart, from the core of a person's being is one that will inspire change. There is nothing more powerful.

The following visualisation will help you create your own vision.

Revisit your Magical Lake. Perhaps *everything* in your lake will form the basis for your vision, or maybe it will be just one element.

Next, find yourself a nice quiet space where you won't be disturbed.

Perhaps, you are sitting in a comfy chair with your feet placed firmly on the floor or maybe you are lying on your bed. Once there and you know you are comfortable you may wish to close your eyes (obviously reading to the end of the exercise before you do so!) and let your breathing settle.

Take a few slow deep breaths in and out. If you can try and lengthen your inhale and exhale, to the count of four, six or eight. Do this a few times and then when you feel ready, just let your breath soften and return to its natural rhythm.

As you do so, consider your vision. Once you have this, start to imagine an image of what life will be like when you have achieved your vision.

What can you see?

What can you hear?

What can you feel?

And as you start to enjoy the moment, imagine you are sat in a large cinema watching the scene play out on the screen in front of you. Turn up the control so the colours become more vivid and bright. Increase the sound so you can hear every nuance of noise and let the feelings you are experiencing envelop your whole being.

Allow the image to become bigger, all-encompassing. When you are comfortable, step into the scene—no longer a spectator but actually able to enjoy the very experience of your vision.

Notice everything that is happening, revel in this glory that is your vision. How are you feeling?

And now that you are *in it* what are you seeing and hearing?

Enjoy the moment and allow it to touch every part of your being. Stay as long as you like, as long as you need and only when you are ready slowly bring yourself back to the cinema, back to your seat.

Rest a while and, when you feel able, start to take a few deeper breaths. Open your eyes and bring yourself back to the present moment.

Fantastic job, you have just embodied your vision.

Find The Es-scale-lator *in the set of scales and write down your vision. Be as detailed and specific as you can.*

The vision is now an integral part of your being. Next time you speak about it, those listening will know it comes from the core of who you are. You will inspire yourself and others because as we all know you are amazingly fantastic.

Powered by gratitude, the es-scale-lator is slow, very slow. No matter how much gratitude there is out there it isn't sufficient to move all the fish in a timely manner. Not only that, but this latest creation only allows for one fish to be moved at a time and only up onto the first branch of the tree. There are no opportunities for the individual fish to share their vision of the lake.

Unfortunately, if the fish are unable to share what they want, the chances of them actually reaching the lake are greatly diminished. They have to be able to share what they desire.

There has to be a solution which will enable them to build on the good work of the es-scale-lator.

CHAPTER SEVEN

THE EEL-LAVATOR

It's a horrible feeling when you walk into a room and the conversation stops.

No matter what people may have been discussing, you're sure it relates to you in some way and immediately your inner critic comes to say hello, highlighting all those limiting beliefs and negative thoughts you hold about yourself.

When we find ourselves in that situation, we are convinced people are talking about us. We dive straight into drama mode, telling ourselves the most outrageous stories and ensuring we take on the role of victim.

Whilst there may be every chance our gut instinct is correct, and the chatter did relate to us, it is just as likely we could be wrong. The only way to find out for sure is to be brave and ask the question, "What were you saying?"

I once worked for an IT software company with the most toxic culture I have ever experienced in my working life. It was as though Maleficent had moved on from putting curses on teenage girls and brought her particular brand of evil into the digital age.

"Yet again I was right. I told you I didn't believe the organisation was what it seemed." Oh hello, my inner critic is back again.

"How lovely, I didn't expect to hear from you again so soon."

"Yes, well I suppose it shows how much I look out for you. I knew you were desperate to find a new job, but you really should listen to me more. Remember, trust is a greatly undervalued quality."

"Mmm," I reply firmly, hitting the mute button.

The Eel-lavator is the answer. It builds on the strengths of the es-scale-lator and has the facility to move the fish higher up the tree, not just to the first branch. This extra movement is creating opportunities for the fish to share their vision.

As one of the fish not invited onto the Eel-lavator, you can only stand and watch as your fellow fish are transported higher up into the tree. Whilst you are happy for them, you can't help wondering what you did wrong. Why you weren't one of the *chosen* fish?

Without an answer, feelings of self-doubt are starting to invade your soft body and you are beginning to question everything you do.

I had known the MD of the IT company for many years. When it was just a tiny start-up business, I took a punt and began using their software. It was a decision I never regretted, until I decided to jump ship and join their organisation.

As the business grew from strength to strength my team began using more of their products. We loved what they did, and their customer service was fantastic. Ok, so our account manager used to change like the weather, but we put that down to the fact the business was growing so fast.

If ever we had a niggle, we would put a call into the MD or one of the people who had been with the company since the beginning and, hey presto, our problem would be resolved!

I was so excited as I drove up the M1 towards my new office. Fortunately, I wasn't going past the Watford Gap, so I felt confident I wouldn't be entering some bizarre and weird world where they would welcome me by saying "Ayup Chuck!"

Little did I know this new environment would give me far more to worry about than northern idiosyncratic sayings I didn't understand.

My first day in this microcosm of technology was a whirlwind of new people, new terminology and new dynamics. It was exciting and scary in equal measures. For many years I had been told the private sector was so much more efficient than the quasi-public-sector environment I had been part of.

I very quickly learnt, it wasn't any better, just different. However, we love to label our assumptions. The private sector is *good and dynamic*, the public sector is *ineffective and wasteful*. Statements, which are simultaneously true and false and therefore totally unhelpful. Yet still we love to use them.

Adjusting to this different world, a term I kept hearing was the *inner circle*. It was only ever spoken in hushed tones and before people uttered the words, they would look over their shoulder to ensure no one was listening and they weren't being watched.

Shrouded in mystery, the *inner circle* sparked my imagination. Was it some religious cult that brainwashed people, a coven of witches who plotted evil spells on their customers, or a group of magicians who could make us do weird things like running around the office completely naked, purely for their own amusement?

When I asked others what it meant, they looked at me smugly and told me they couldn't say, I would figure it out soon enough. It felt like a rite of passage.

The inner circle was in fact a very small group of people who had the MD's ear. They spent hours locked away together. The problem was all the meeting rooms had glass doors and windows, so the entire company could see them. It was always the same four or five people. Occasionally other people were asked in, but this didn't happen very often and not for very long.

I finally understood people's reticence in sharing what they knew about the inner circle. Was I to be included or excluded? Having been brought in as their first ever externally appointed director nobody was sure what was going to happen.

It transpired I was to be let in but only for a little while. When it became clear I wasn't comfortable in an environment which was so elitist, I was cast aside and only invited back in when it was absolutely necessary.

What did I learn about the inner circle? Well for those who were in it, they relished their position. It gave them certain privileges that weren't afforded to other people. They could come and go as they pleased and when they failed to meet a deadline, they blamed it on someone who was outside the *inner circle*.

For some reason it was completely acceptable for those within the circle to not hit deadlines but totally unacceptable for those who were outside. Once again unhelpful labels were applied to those people, "He's lazy / She's stupid / He hasn't got a clue." A tactic designed to ensure those inside the circle could feel even more entitled to look down on the mere *minions* who formed the other part of the organisation.

Those in the inner circle adorned themselves with beautiful robes made of the finest materials, silk and cashmere. Brightly coloured, these vestments were tailored precisely to the size and shape of the person who wore them. Some robes had gilt edges whilst others had the most precious stones, rubies and diamonds embedded within them.

Meanwhile those who could only glance in were dressed in dull and dreary rags and the occasional random tarpaulin. Their faded, ill-fitting clothes also had tears and rips due to their age and the amount of washing they had undergone. Many of the garments were made of the cheapest materials which caused irritation, so the only colour which could be seen was the red of the sores on people's skin.

The chasm between the two groups was heartbreaking and sickening.

Those in rags were demotivated and disinterested. Sickness levels were atrocious and staff turnover was sky-high. Was it any wonder? When 70 people shared one office and there was an inner circle of just five why would it be any different? This toxic culture not only devastated the people working within the business but also its poor customers.

The fish invited to use the eel-lavator are all very similar. Angel fish, they are brightly coloured blues and yellows and together they create an illusion of the sun rising high above the bright blue sea. They are beautiful and alluring. There is not a blob fish amongst them.

However, you realise their behaviour is at odds with their beauty. By only allowing fish *like them* on to the eel-lavator they are excluding many more. Ordinary looking fish like you and me. Fish that may not be as aesthetically pleasing but have much to offer; other skills that could be put to good use for the greater good of all fish not just a select few.

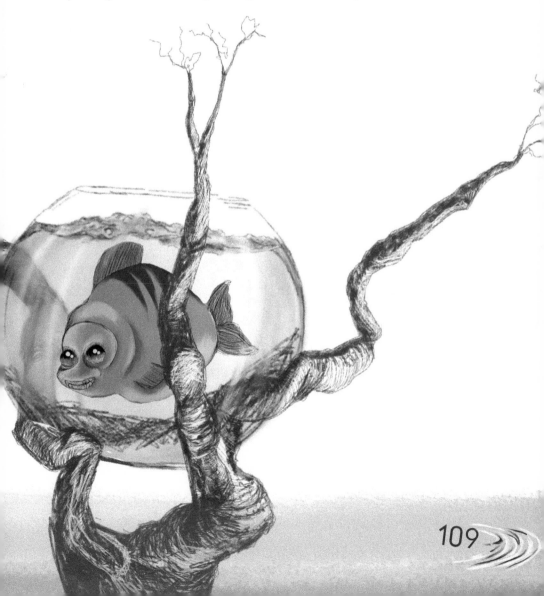

As children we loved to play the game *Chinese Whispers*.

Sitting in a circle with our friends one of us would start with a sentence, which we would whisper into the ear of the person who was sat next to us. This person would then whisper the same sentence into the ear of the person next to them and so the game would continue until it came to the last person

The final person would then say the message out loud. The message at the start and the finish never matched. Not even once. Occasionally there might be a slight correlation between the two but not very often.

As a child I played this game, my children played this game and unbelievably it's a game I sometimes play with my clients. Just because we grow up into fully functioning, mature, responsible adults, does not mean we learn how to stop the Chinese Whispers.

In my experience, when you don't include people, they will make up their own stories and start their own game of Chinese Whispers. Like the time I heard about a colleague who was going to be sacked for gross misconduct, when they had only been delivering a form to HR.

Or the girl from accounts who had found out she was pregnant and then been dumped by her boyfriend, when in fact she had been crying tears of joy telling her manager she had just got engaged. Or the office cat who became a witch at night and cast wicked spells over those people who hadn't stroked it the previous day.

Fact. What we don't know we will make up.

And as the story is passed on so it will become more imaginative and eventful. Now, if you are a drama queen like my daughter Louisa, this may be a very useful skill, but in a work environment it is destructive and divisive.

For a moment, I'd like you to consider whether you have an inner circle at work. Are you part of such a group or have you created one?

If not, I am sure you have your go-to people. The people you trust. The ones you know you can rely on. If you ask them to do something it will get done.

It makes sense doesn't it? Why would you ask someone else, when you know they won't complete the job?

On one level it seems like a completely sensible approach to have your go-to people, but have you ever considered what impact your behaviour will be having on other people, your team, your colleagues?

Treat people as if they are outside the *circle*, dressed in dull and dreary rags, and over time they will start to behave in a way which is in keeping with this. Behaviour breeds behaviour.

"I'm sorry, but why should I believe a word you are saying? I have been a customer for years and the service we receive from you guys is rubbish. You never deliver anything on time and whilst you are all lovely to deal with, we don't trust you. We never speak to the same person twice and you charge us for every change you make."

Another client visit, another very unhappy customer.

I had joined the IT company believing the service I had received over the years was the service all their customers enjoyed. My first few client visits blew this idea firmly out the water and it soon became apparent my experience had been the exception not the rule. There was also an inner circle of customers.

Unlike the employees, clients within the inner circle had no clue they had been placed there or that those outside of it were having a dramatically different experience.

During my short time with the organisation (this time there was no waiting around to let the toxicity get me to such a dark place, inertia felt like the only option) I realised the minions weren't minions at all. They were just being set up to fail. They were desperate to do a good job and were constantly swimming against the tide to stay afloat. Given the environment it was an almost impossible task.

With so few managing so many, the direction of travel changed like the wind. Every few weeks, new departments were being created to capitalise on the latest idea, people's job titles were changed as if that would enable them to do their job more effectively. Strategy and planning were non-existent.

Everything was lastminute.com and those clients who created themostnoise.com went to the top of the to-do pile until someone else shouted louder and usurpedtheirposition.com.

It was completely and utterly bananas and all because the MD chose to rely on a select few and believed the others were almost surplus to requirements. Can you imagine being in such a destructive environment?

When you have a vision for yourself, your team, your organisation, the temptation is always to share it with those you are closest to, those you trust, those who see the world as you do.

The problem is, with this approach you are in danger of creating an inner circle and alienating all those outside it. It is also foolhardy to believe a vision which encapsulates everyone can be achieved by communicating with just a few.

*In the set of scales use **The Eel-lavator** to consider who are the people in your inner circle and who are those in the outer circle.*

Organisations often make this mistake. They have a bold and brave vision for the future, but they forget to communicate it effectively. There may be an all staff email announcing the new words of wisdom or even the odd presentation or two but there isn't the time or effort spent on embodying it so every person in the organisation can hear it, see it, feel it.

For many, osmosis is the preferred method of communicating vision and values. This might work when a business is small. The MD has a clear vision for their business. As the first person joins the organisation, they are able to decipher what this is by closely observing the MD's behaviour, listening to what he says and watching how he behaves.

This may also work for the next person who is recruited and the one after that, but it soon becomes an ineffective method of communication because just like Chinese Whispers the message gets lost in translation.

The MD becomes frustrated people aren't seeing what he sees and the people themselves are just confused because there is no clear direction and they have no idea whether what they are doing fits with the higher plan.

It's a recipe for disaster and one that plays out in many organisations irrespective of their size.

Even the fish in the eel-lavator are starting to recognise their plan might not be working. Sure, they are surrounded by fish who are just *like them*, but they are not making the progress they thought they would. Whilst the eel-lavator can move fish higher up the tree, it can only do so one fish and one branch at a time.

The fish recognise they need something better than the eel-lavator. Something that will enable them to travel together and move up the tree more quickly than one branch at a time.

Out of ideas and realising they might be about to fail they invite some of the *less* beautiful fish into the discussions about how they can improve the eel-lavator.

Many of the fish stay silent, scared of speaking up, fearful of ridicule. However, one brave soul decides to share his idea. *Noahshark*, who has been around for over 125 million years, before even dinosaurs existed, pipes up with all the wisdom of a fish who has seen and experienced so much. He suggests the group tries the Exp-wrasse Elevator.

CHAPTER EIGHT

THE EXP-WRASSE ELEVATOR

It was completely black. I could feel the darkness pervading my body like a disease and I couldn't see a thing. Not even a half-hearted or vague form appeared from the inky shroud to help me gather my bearings.

No matter how much I strained my eyes or willed myself to see even a glimmer of light, I couldn't. The noise surrounding me was loud and overwhelming. I was terrified and I wanted to scream, but knew I couldn't.

We are told when we lose one of our senses the other four compensate for the loss. We assume this is a good reaction. We lose our sense of smell, so our sense of taste becomes much greater, enabling us to savour every single ingredient in the mouthful of food we are tasting.

What if this isn't the case?

What if by removing one of our senses those remaining become more sensitive, creating an unnerving and scary environment?

Alone in the dark, I had not been kidnapped by some terror gang who had thrown me into the cellar of a haunted house in the middle of nowhere demanding a huge ransom from my loving family, but was instead, sat in a restaurant in central London.

A restaurant called *Dans Le Noir*. It offers diners the experience of eating in a room which is completely dark. And all the waiters are blind.

When something goes wrong, we typically look for someone to blame. This is especially true in the workplace. If there is a failure in service, we need to identify the person or team responsible. If there is a reduction in sales, then quite obviously there is a problem with the sales team. And if an organisation has had a string of bad recruits, then it is most definitely the fault of HR and the recruiting manager.

And whilst the focus is on finding the person or people to blame, we can deflect the attention away from us. We can tell ourselves we had no part in this activity which had failed in some way. We can choose not to look in the mirror and ask ourselves the question, "What was my contribution?"

We all hate this blame culture and yet it is endemic in the workplace. I am yet to meet anyone who says "Mel, what is a blame culture? I have never worked in a business with one."

In my experience the blame culture in organisations exists for two reasons: fear and trust. Fear, because employees are fearful of owning up when they've made a mistake and the consequences they will endure as a result. And trust because they do not trust the organisation will deal with their error in a fair and reasonable manner.

If you asked managers what they would do if a member of their team made a mistake, the majority would respond with statements such

as, "It's an opportunity to learn / We all make mistakes / None of us are perfect."

None of these responses should evoke fear or mistrust in an employee. So why is there such a difference between what managers say they do and reality?

It's working, the Exp-wrasse Elevator. Many more fish are being transported around the tree and their movement is not limited to one branch at a time. The fish can choose to move up several branches at a time. Many of them are aiming to get to the top, enticed by the fruit but also eager to learn whether from this vantage point they will be able to see the beautiful lake.

What a wonderful invention this exp-wrasee elevator is, allowing fish to travel where they want.

Dan, our waiter, had warned us we might find the dining experience overwhelming. On arrival at the restaurant, François, the tall and debonair maître d', advised us in the most wonderful French accent we would need to place all our belongings in a locker before entering the restaurant as there could not be any trip hazards in the dining room.

We happily obliged and took our seat in the bar area. A grand room with tall ceilings. It had a unique feel to it: high-end Victorian luxury crossed with French chic bistro. Velvet covered sofas in opulent greens and reds were combined with quirky oak coffee tables.

The excitement in the room was palpable and the mix of clientele wide ranging. Students in jeans and Dr Martens alongside family groups and those people who still liked to dress up for dinner. In some ways it was an unusual mix, but we all had one thing in common. A desire to try out a unique dining experience.

François asked us to take our place in the corridor just outside the dining room, alongside six other people. Our trepidation was mounting, just as it does when you are waiting in the queue to do something completely out of your comfort zone, like riding a scary roller coaster, zip wiring across the Thames or waiting for surgery to remove nasal chips.

No matter how you are feeling, you are determined to go through with it no matter what.

Dan appeared and asked us to stand facing him in a line and put our right hand on the person's shoulder in front. Already this was a very uncomfortable feeling, creating physical contact with someone we didn't know. Nervous laughter bubbled up from some of us.

"I am going to be leading you to your table," Dan said. "Please ensure you keep your hand on the shoulder of the person in front and follow my instructions." With that he made his way along the line asking our names, skilfully having a bit of banter with each of us, building rapport and helping calm us down.

Dan was short with dark curly hair. He had an air of fun about him, someone who would always be a good party guest with his bon viveur personality and innate caring nature. It was easy to imagine Dan suggesting, oh so tactfully, to someone who was slightly inebriated that they replace their vodka with water.

Back at the front of our line once more, he gently took the lead person's hand and asked, "Are you ready to start moving forward?"

"Yes", we all replied loudly, eager to get going.

"Ok, let's do this. Some of you may find it intimidating when we first get into the dining room. Please don't worry, it's perfectly normal. If you do feel a little strange, just take a few moments and focus on your breathing."

By this point I am not sure how many of us were truly listening, we were just keen to get in there. Personally, I was thinking, I have been in dark places before (my inner critic takes me there all the time), how hard can this really be?

When I became director at the University of Studymore, the maintenance team was moved across into my newly created department, so once again Robert and I were working together. In truth, the team had never received much love and attention from senior management, so Robert was left to his own devices.

After all maintenance was only the section people called upon when something went wrong—a blocked toilet, a failed heating system, or when, for no apparent reason whatsoever, a student's bedroom door bizarrely ended up off its hinges.

A team, who sorted out all these issues but was never adequately respected or appreciated for the work they did. Neither did they believe they had sufficient manpower or resource to deal with the myriad of calls they received. This team needed my attention and so I decided to take radical action.

Based down the bottom end of campus, the maintenance domain was one few chose to enter willingly. If people were forced to visit, they did not stay long and left as quickly as they could.

The maintenance workshop was a prefab building, dull and grey. Just walking up to it you could feel it sapping away your energy. There was no warmth or welcoming features. Imagine coming to work every morning and walking into such a building. It was hardly an environment which would inspire people to do their best.

Nonetheless, I decided to make this my new home.

The team were very accommodating and moved around to make room for me. I was given a tiny corner office at the front of the building. It was functional and the view out of my window is one people would have died for.

Gone was my office in a Grade I listed building overlooking a beautiful quadrangle of well-tended lawns and coloured stone pathways: replaced instead with a view of huge grey metal storage containers on one side and across from my office door the men's toilets!

Having made the decision to swap beautiful orange stonework for grey pebble-dash and Victorian luxury for flat-pack functionality there was only one thing I could do.

Add colour.

As one of only a very small number of women inhabiting this male environment I decided to pay homage to my soul colour. Pink.

We agreed one of the walls in my office was to be painted pink and then on a whim we took the decision my office door should be the same colour as well. Whilst I was still safely ensconced in Victorian luxury, Robert asked one of his painters, Fred, to come and find me so we could choose the exact colour.

The moment Fred stepped into my office I could tell by the look on his face he thought I was off my trolley. "Uh Mel, I've been sent up with the colour charts, so you can choose what you want for your office."

"Fantastic," I replied excitedly, "Let's have a look."

Clearly pink was not a colour which was in high demand from a trade perspective. Imagining the colour palette would please any rainbow unicorn and be similar to the choice B&Q offered me when I was painting my house, I envisaged agonising over the exact shade for hours. I was a little disappointed to realise this was not going to be the case.

I had the option of just two colours. Stoically, after three seconds of intense contemplation, I chose my preferred colour (which was more cold flesh than hot pink). Fred left still convinced I was bonkers, saying my office would be ready in a week's time.

Another phone call from Robert, this time not asking for my help but chuckling down the phone, asking when I had some time to go visit my new office.

The noise was deafening. We sensed there were people all around us and yet we couldn't see them. Slowly, we were putting one foot in front of the other. Dan brought us to a stop and took four people to their table. We could hear him carefully giving instructions, helping each of them to find their seats. Once he knew they were safe and settled he left saying, "I'll be back in a little while."

We were on the move again and this time, Dan helped us to our seats. He instructed me to stay where I was whilst he guided my friend to her place. He then came back and gave me very clear instructions to find my seat and get settled. I was in awe of his skills because in that moment we were both blind and yet I was totally reliant on him.

"Hello, I'm John," said a friendly voice that seemed to be coming from the left of me. "Oh," I thought. "We're on a table with other people. Strangers I don't know, and I can't see."

"Hi, I'm Mel and this is my friend, Nishma." I replied as cheerfully as I could.

It turned out John was there with his wife Nicole and their two good friends Sam and Delilah. Everyone started chatting, but I fell silent. The overwhelm Dan had warned us about hit me hard. I was desperately trying to see but I just couldn't.

It was true my hearing had heightened but not in the good way I imagined it would. Instead I could hear every nuance of noise, the scrape of a chair and the sound of a nail being nervously bitten, which rather than being comforting was extremely intimidating. I started to feel sick, and a bit panicked.

"Breathe, breathe," I told myself, thinking back to what Dan had said. I was squeezing the table hard. It was solid and reliable and about the only thing I knew I could count on in this unfamiliar world I had entered. Eventually, as Dan predicted, the breathing did help and I slowly adjusted to my surroundings although I was still straining my eyes, desperate to be able to see something.

Finally, I gave up the battle and accepted for the next couple of hours my existence was going to be completely different as I adjusted to life without sight.

Fish are being injured and hurt.

In their excitement to try out this new mode of transport, which will take them wherever they want to go in the tree, fish are launching themselves onto the exp-wrasse elevator, without any thought for who else might be using it.

With no coordination, fish are bumping bowls and vying for the position which will enable them to get to the top of the tree first. As a result some of the fish are being hurt, but instead of recognising how their own behaviour has contributed to their injury, they immediately look for someone else to blame.

Those who are not as forceful are waiting patiently at the side, looking around for someone to take control of the situation and sort it out. Many look to *Noahshark* for guidance, but he just raises his elongated snout and drops it down again, not interested in giving advice. He wants the fish to find their own solution.

Use The Exp-wrasse Elevator *in the set of scales to consider the situations when you have blamed other people.*

Robert met me outside the grey monstrosity that was going to be my new home. He was a tall man at six-foot four, very excitable and reminded me of Tigger as he bounded around.

"Come on, let me show you what we've done," said Robert.

Inside, he announced painting my door pink had inspired the team. They liked the idea of coloured doors if not *soul* pink and decided to paint every door in the building a different colour. And alongside the coloured door each room now had a feature wall of colour.

One office was even going to have its own piece of bespoke artwork. Carpenter Dave was also purported to be a talented artist so Robert asked him to go crazy and create his own version of wall art. Although it wasn't yet complete it was a fantastic reflection of his creativity and an untapped skill we didn't even know he possessed.

By the end of the tour I was ecstatic and wanted to give Robert a massive kiss but of course that would have been highly inappropriate and so instead I smiled broadly and said, "This is going to be such great fun."

"People have their own lives and I don't want to be a burden."

It was nearly the end of our evening at *Dans le Noir* and Nishma and I were chatting with Dan. The restaurant had quietened down and we were finding out more about what it was really like to be a blind person.

Before taking this job, Dan had worked for BT doing admin. We were thoroughly in awe of what he did and told him so. Completely unassuming, Dan didn't see what he was doing was anything special or inspirational. We begged to differ.

Nishma asked Dan what it was like living in London and whether people were as helpful to him as he had been to us. "People are busy, so I get they might not be able to stop and help me," he said. There was no trace of bitterness in his voice, Dan was just explaining the situation. We

couldn't believe how understanding he was of those people who chose to walk round him rather than help him.

As Dan was speaking, I was imagining what it must be like to walk along a busy London street, with your hearing heightened to such an extent the noise is not comforting but alarming. And then stopping and waiting to cross the road. Knowing there are people around you who are too busy with their own lives to help.

In that moment I caught a glimpse of how awful we can be as human beings. No one was being killed or tortured or stabbing a stranger to discover their humanity again—atrocities we associate with the worst of human behaviour. But not stopping to help a blind man cross the road because we are too busy with our own lives is just as shameful.

Had I not experienced what life was really like for a blind person, I wouldn't have had that realisation. But fortunately, I did, and the understanding will stay with me forever.

Chatting with Dan was the highlight of what had been a completely life-changing evening. I also realised how profound the proverb is, "Don't judge a man until you have walked a mile in his shoes."

I was aware then just how naïve my thinking had been. I was ashamed of all those times I had previously sat in project boards for new university buildings, assuming that if we met the requirements of the Disability Discrimination Act, we would be sufficiently accommodating the needs of those with specific disabilities. How foolhardy and ignorant.

I had no clue, no real understanding. Feeling totally overawed by the noise around me. Eating dinner with my fingers because it was impossible to get any food into my mouth using cutlery. Spilling a drink I couldn't see taught me, as someone who was fortunate enough to have their sight, I had no clue what life was like for a visually impaired person. My perception was miles away from reality.

The maintenance team was underperforming on all levels. Team morale was at an all-time low, sickness levels were through the roof and the service level agreement targets were only being achieved eighteen percent of the time. This was a team in crisis and something needed to change.

As director I had a sense of what might be going on below the surface but despite many conversations with Robert we couldn't identify the root cause and so we agreed to bring in some external support to help get to the bottom of what was driving this poor performance.

We called on the help of my coach who had also coached Robert. We asked her to come and be part of the team for a week. Harriet went out on jobs, sat in on team meetings and generally had a good old rummage around the department, people and processes. She even had a good look through the pot plants we had placed at the front of the building.

Three days in, there was a knock on my door and Harriet came in looking worried. We took a seat on the brightly coloured beanbags, green for Harriet and of course pink for me.

"I'm pretty sure I know what the root problem is," said Harriet getting straight to the point.

"Oh yes?"

"Yes, it's Robert. Of course, there are lots of other issues but the main one is Robert. He is not leading his team as he should."

Harriet's words shocked me, but not as much as you might have expected. Over the months I had been working with Robert, I had a sense he was part of the problem but hadn't realised how fundamental his contribution was. We chatted about her findings and agreed we needed to meet with Robert.

Sat in the same room, where we had previously celebrated our efforts in getting consensus to move forward with the proposed working patterns for the maintenance team, the atmosphere on this occasion was very different.

Delivered with tough love, Harriet ran through her findings with Robert. Having spent a week with the team, she was able to give clear examples where Robert wasn't listening or demonstrating good management behaviour. Most telling was his preference to be off-site doing other *fun* things, which did not involve him looking after his business function or team.

Watching the interaction play out, I could tell Harriet's findings came as a shock to Robert, that he'd been unaware of his behaviour and the impact it was having. At times his deep blue eyes widened in astonishment. His shoulders began to sag and he was finding it hard to make eye contact. It was the most hard-hitting message I have ever seen delivered but it was done with absolute love and compassion.

The meeting wasn't about giving Robert a dressing down or laying the blame at his door. It was about holding up a mirror for Robert to look into. So that he could, for the first time in his life, really have a good look at himself as a leader. To see the wrinkles and the blemishes but also the smooth areas and the multitude of tones that made up his skin. To look beyond the colour of his eyes and see deep into his soul.

And having done this, consider whether he was happy with what he saw. Did he want to make any changes? Harriet and I assured Robert we would help him in any way we could. But first he needed to process everything he had seen in the mirror.

Tigger had entered the room, but it was a tired and weary tiger that left. It was the most difficult meeting of my career, but I knew we had done the right thing. As hard as it had been for us to deliver the message it had been much harder for Robert to receive it. And not giving

Robert the full picture would have been unfair. At least now he had the opportunity to decide what he wanted to do.

"Do you think he will come in tomorrow?" I asked Harriet.

"I honestly don't know," she replied. "I am not sure I would, but it's his choice."

I agreed. Neither of us had ever walked in Robert's shoes so why would we imagine we could know what he would do.

Organisations have an obligation to create environments which will enable their people to thrive. Managers have a responsibility to help their team fulfil their potential.

Admirable statements, but it doesn't often happen.

People excel in their operational role and we decide to promote them. We assume that because *Person A* was a fantastic administrator, they would make a fabulous office manager. We tell them the good news, we promote them, and we pat ourselves on the back for a job well done because we have recruited from within.

In amongst all the good will and celebration we neglect to do the one most important thing. We forget to ensure *Person A* has the right skills to be just as fantastic in the role of office manager as they were in their administrator position.

And so, despite our very best intentions to do good we set someone up to fail rather than succeed. This is most definitely not a do-good action. And of course, when they fail, we blame them entirely, failing to see that their failure is down to us not them. We refuse to look in the mirror.

By holding up a mirror, Harriet and I had presented Robert with an opportunity to consider his own behaviour. However, we also needed to consider our own actions. Had we delivered the message in the best way possible? Could we have chosen a different approach?

Stephen Covey says, "We judge ourselves by our intentions and others by their behaviour."

Harriet and I were confident with how we addressed the situation but perhaps you would have chosen to tackle it differently. The reality is when we are dealing with people there are always numerous options. And the choice we make will depend on the circumstances, the people involved and the outcome we want to achieve.

Robert had a management role, but at the time, he was not leading or managing his team in a way that was either effective or inspiring.

However, it was not only Robert who needed to look in the mirror. So did I. As his line manager I needed to ask myself the question, "Was there more I could have done to support his development so the maintenance team had not ended up in that dark and depressing place?"

And that mirror did not just need to be held up to me but also all the other people who had been part of Robert's journey. Failure is very rarely the responsibility of one person, no matter what we may tell ourselves.

The number of accidents is on the increase. Not only that but the injuries are gradually becoming more serious. The fish are forming groups, looking to blame others for their current circumstances. Unwilling to confront what is really happening, they prefer to focus their attention on other groups and their inappropriate use of the exp-wrasse elevator.

No longer able to just stay back and let the drama unfold, *Noahshark* decides to help the other fish by introducing them to the Cod-seerge. Cod-seerge offers a special service. She will not solve their problems. But if the fish are willing to engage with her, they may be able to find the answers they have been looking for.

CHAPTER NINE

COD-SEERGE SERVICE

"I am sorry," he said as his voice cracked with emotion. "I have let you all down and I need to apologise."

He lifted his gaze slowly from the floor and made eye contact with each of the three people in the room. There were tears in his eyes. "Things are going to change. I hope you will give me a chance to put things right." He dropped his head once again, trying to regain his composure.

It was the morning after Robert been given a mirror to take a long hard look at himself. Following an early morning chat with Harriet, he had asked myself and his senior management to join him in the same room that was becoming synonymous with the highs and lows of an emotional roller coaster.

Whilst the previous day the message had been the most hard-hitting I had ever experienced, the conversation the following morning was the most heartfelt. Both had been delivered with the utmost love and compassion. It was a touching twist to the previous day's deeply wounding scars.

Robert's team received his apology with grace and in that moment of outright openness a bond was created between them which was so strong not even Iron Man would have been able to pull it apart.

As human beings one of the biggest misconceptions we have is the belief that we can change other people. We believe if we badger someone constantly, they will change. If we provide work colleagues with training, they will change. If people have a heart attack, they will change their lifestyle.

Wrong. Wrong. Wrong.

The only person who can change me is me. The only person who can change you is you.

So why do we choose to ignore this truth and keep trying to change other people. Because life would be so much easier if we could. My partner would be on time, my kids would pick their clothes up from the bedroom floor and my parents would finally realise I was no longer a six-year-old girl with pigtails and a penchant for sparkly tights.

What does this mean from an organisational perspective? Well certainly it helps us to understand why 70% of change projects fail and for some it may well cause them to question the need to change. If the chances of success are so small, why bother?

The answer is simple, change is inevitable.

If businesses choose not to change or adapt to market conditions, customer demands or technological advances, they will wither and eventually die. Trampled on by competitors who are eager to change, who find strategies to ensure their programmes are part of the 30% that are successful.

Imagine your life ten years from now. Not a single element had changed. You hadn't been to a different holiday destination, changed your car or even the cushions on your sofa. Do you think you would be happy?

No.

Therefore, change is inescapable. The question is not, do we have to change? But, how can we change successfully?

Having been introduced to Cod-seerge, some of the fish decide to turn their backs on her and swim as far away as possible. They are happy to believe their actions are right and it's only ever the other fish who are wrong.

Some of the braver ones decide to give Cod-seerge's service a go, especially as *Noahshark* had recommended it. After all, this is a fish who has been around for millions of years, so he must know what he is talking about, right?

Holding up the mirror, Harriet and I were able to create a pivotal moment for Robert. He had a choice to make about the person he wanted to be. Did he want to be an effective manager or an inspiring leader, a mix of the two or something entirely different?

He could also choose to carry on as he had before ignoring all that he had seen. He could run away and pretend the mirror moment had never happened or he could choose to be brave and make some changes.

Robert chose to be a brave and courageous warrior. He chose to return to the university and he chose to change his behaviour. Had I been able to I would have given him a medal in recognition of his bravery and honesty, and to honour the heartfelt apology he gave his team.

Never underestimate the fortitude of someone wishing to make a change to their behaviour. It is rarely as simple as flicking a switch because as we know the drivers of our behaviour are sat in the big chunk of our behavioural iceberg we cannot see.

To change our behaviour takes grit and determination and the journey is very rarely an easy one. It is never smooth and straight but full of twists and turns with hazards flying at us from all angles trying to derail our progress.

Having decided to spend time with Cod-seerge, the fish realise what an extraordinary service she offers. By holding up a magic mirror, Cod-seerge enables the fish to see themselves for the very first time, in all their fish glory. As well as providing a magic mirror, Cod-seerge also offers the gift of feedback so the fish can, for the first time, understand how they are viewed by their fellow fish.

This combined service enables the fish to not only observe their physical beauty but, more importantly, look deep inside themselves: to understand and take responsibility for their behaviour.

They no longer expect someone else to take control of the exp-wrasse elevator. If they choose to use it then they must take accountability for their own actions.

Have you ever looked in the mirror like Robert did? Not to admire your good looks, check your hair is ok or ensure your lipstick hasn't smudged. But to look into your eyes, deep into your soul, to see if there are aspects of your being you would like to change.

If not, I would challenge you to have a go.

Sit in front of a mirror and bring your attention to your eyes. For a moment you may wish to close them whilst you take a few deep, calming breaths, quietening the internal chatter taking place inside your head.

Do this for as long as you need. When you feel able to, look into the mirror, into your eyes. Send yourself as much love as you can,

knowing that this exercise is coming from a place of compassion and self-care. Once you have done this allow your gaze to soften, all the while sending yourself love and care.

And when you are ready, start to talk with the person in front of you, listing everything you love about them, all those traits that make you smile and should be celebrated. Be as effusive and as loving as you can.

When you have no more to say, with as much love and kindness as you have within you, gently speak of those actions which can be unhelpful to the person you are looking at. Those behaviours that can hold them back from being totally amazingly brilliant.

Accept this gift of feedback willingly, knowing that is coming from someone who only wants the best for you and it is your choice what you do with it. A gift that has been given lovingly should also be received in the same vein.

Thank the person you see in the mirror for giving you the time and space to be able to do this. And with complete joy in your heart and mind close your eyes again.

Relish the experience and the learning. When you are ready take a few deep breaths to bring yourself back into the present moment. Open your eyes and congratulate yourself for a job well done.

In the set of scales, find **The Cod-seerge Service** *and note down everything you have discovered about yourself in the mirror. On the Cod-seerge's name badge note down any feedback you have received about yourself, both the elements that should be celebrated and those which are slightly uncomfortable.*

With this combined knowledge, write in the fishbowl what you plan to do as a result, accepting that you are responsible for your behaviour.

I was thirty-three years old when I first had my experience of coaching. Having just returned from maternity to a job I loved, I felt out of kilter with the world as if my feet could not hold me steady. In the time I had been away we had acquired a new training manager and somehow (perhaps because he was totally awesome at what he did) he knew I could do with a little bit of help.

Sat in my office of Victorian decadence (I hadn't yet moved up to the world of flat-pack functionality), drinking coffee and planning the next departmental away day, Kwame suddenly said, "I've been thinking about your personal development."

"Oh yes," I replied, slightly shocked he didn't have better things to do like count the number of whiteboard pens he had in his training drawer.

"How would you feel about having some coaching?"

"What, you mean, you want to take me on a coach drive?" Ok, so maybe I didn't exactly say that, but it was the first time I had ever heard the term and I really had no clue what it meant.

"Coaching is an up-and-coming development tool mainly aimed at top executives. I thought you could really benefit from it. What do you think?"

Having had no personal development up until that point in my career, I jumped at the opportunity as Kwame knew I would. He explained the development journey would involve six one-to-one sessions with my coach. To get us started on the journey Kwame would also ask her to carry out some 360-degree feedback with my peers, direct reports, manager and members of the university SMT.

A few weeks later sat in a different room which was across the quadrangle from my usual home, I was embarking on my first formal coaching session with Anita who I had met and concluded I could work

with. I walked in as one version of Mel and left feeling completely different.

Walking back along the quadrangle, I felt like skipping and swinging my arms in the air. Although it was a dull grey day all I saw was bright sunshine and blue sky. Something had shifted in my psyche and I knew there was no going back. Instead of heading for my office, I went and found Kwame to thank him for the most unexpected gift I had ever been given.

In those two hours with Anita, I not only heard wonderful feedback about my performance (she said that it was the best feedback she had ever received about anyone she had ever worked with), I also realised that the only person that was holding me back was me. Grasping that concept was a life-changing moment.

Nowadays, coaching has become a mainstream development tool and it can be immensely powerful in helping individuals and teams change their behaviour. However, it can only be effective if the coachee is willing to make adjustments.

Robert was desperate to become a better manager and so Harriet and I worked with him to pull together a development strategy which would enable him to achieve his goal. The plan was multi-layered, not just offering him coaching but other interventions that would support him in developing a team we could all be proud of.

Conscious we were running a business, I was aware we needed to set a target for the planned improvement. Consequently, Robert and I agreed that within six months the achievement of the section's service level agreements will have increased from the current 18% to 75%. This was not an easy to achieve goal but one that would require a radical overhaul of the current operation.

Choosing to change as an individual is hard. Choosing to change as an organisation is out of this world, galaxy and the universe difficult. For an organisation to successfully change, it will need to ensure its people change and that is one to the power of many. To be honest in these circumstances, odds of a thirty percent success rate seem very favourable and I would grab them with both hands.

Often when we are leading change programmes at work we expect people to come on board no matter what. And if people don't react in the way we would like, we label them as disruptive and difficult. We show little or no appreciation for how they may be feeling. Robert's project to change the working hours of his team was a great example of this.

It was 11.38pm on the twenty-third of June, 2016, and we were stood on the platform of Waterloo station, with hundreds of other people, staring intently at the information boards, hoping against hope that we would be able to make it home and into our beds that were loudly calling us.

Having had a wonderful night dancing to *Copacabana* and swaying our arms along to *Mandy* (yes you guessed it, we had been to a Barry Manilow concert), my partner and I were bemused when we got to Waterloo and found we couldn't just jump on a train back to Woking, thanks to a technical fault.

With the adrenaline rush starting to fade and extreme tiredness filling the void, I was in danger of going into full operatic diva mode that would have given Louisa a run for her Valkyrie wings. It was late, I was tired, and I just wanted my bed. What I most definitely did not want was to be standing on the platform waiting to find out if there were going to be any trains.

It just wasn't fair!

Fortunately, South West Trains must have heard about my family's diva moments and so in order to avoid an international incident (my singing voice would have caused even the most easy-going commuter to call MI5) they magic-upped a train so that finally, at half past midnight,

we were on our way home, stopping at every station between Woking and Waterloo.

At the University of Studymore, when maintenance became part of my team, the revised working patterns had been in operation for a year and it was clear they weren't working. The basis for the proposed changes was to improve customer satisfaction, increase productivity and be able to offer a better service.

Unfortunately, none of these aims had been met. Customer complaints were at an all-time high. No more jobs were being *closed* despite the team being there at times when theoretically they should have been able to get into empty buildings and offices and due to the team being demotivated and disgruntled the service had not improved on any level.

As part of Robert's plan to turn things around he knew he would have to address the issue of working patterns. Having not yet recovered from the scars left from the previous three-year battle with his team he was very reluctant to do this. Whilst I completely understood his feelings, I reminded him that as a brave and courageous warrior he could not pick his battles. He had to meet every challenge head on.

The twenty-third of June, 2016, was a day that will forever be etched into the United Kingdom history books. Not because I had finally achieved my lifelong ambition of seeing Bazza in concert, but because it was day the British nation got to have their say about whether they wanted the UK to remain in the EU or leave it.

I had cast my vote earlier in the day and so as the train slowly made its way from Waterloo to Woking I decided to see if any of the counts were in. The first results had been released and confirmed what the pundits had been predicting, the UK would remain in the EU. Armed with this knowledge I turned off my phone and slept the rest of the way home.

The next morning, having walked the kids to school, I was having breakfast with my good friend Victoria who had kindly babysat for me. Chatting away I was about to take a bite of my granary toast when she said, "Mel, you do know what's happened?"

I could tell from the sound of her voice it was something serious, but for the life of me I really couldn't think what. "No," I replied tentatively, slowly putting down my piece of toast.

"We're out."

Victoria didn't have to say any more. The ball had bounced, and I knew exactly what she was referring to.

"Oh my God. You have got to be kidding me. On our way home, last night the first count had voted to remain. I had assumed the final result would be the same."

"Well it didn't stay that way, we are out!"

For the next few moments neither of us said anything, wrapped up in our thoughts. I felt sick and for the shortest of seconds some mad thoughts whizzed through my head. What did this mean for my girls' future? Would the result bring about another economic crisis? Would authentic sangria still be available in my local supermarket?

The questions were endless. But the truth of the matter was there were very few answers and the fear of the unknown increased my anxiety. Victoria and I discussed all sorts of scenarios because as we know, when we don't have facts, we create our own stories to match our view of the world.

I had never believed the result would affect me in this way but over the next couple of days my emotions were all over the place. I was angry at those people who had placed the UK in a situation where the future was not clear, and I was depressed about the legacy that would be left to my children.

In those moments when the red mist cleared, I did start to consider the positives of the situation, but to begin with these moments were few and far between. For the first few days you could not escape the discussion surrounding the result. Just like the debates which had taken place prior to the election it became clear there were views to fit whichever camp you found yourself in.

For those who had voted to leave, they had an overwhelming sense justice had been done and the UK's future was now secure. Those who had voted to remain believed we had just been sent to death row to await our inevitable downfall.

By the Sunday I had had enough of it all. Whichever side you sat on the reality was no one really knew what the future would hold. The only true and definitive fact was the British people had spoken and they had chosen to leave the EU.

Accepting this fact, I realised little old me could not alter the tide of change. I could not influence what subsequent decisions were taken by the UK government and I could not impact how people chose to behave. Therefore, I decided the best I could do was to accept the situation for now and address any future issues as they arose.

Scaremongering or worrying about issues which were beyond my sphere of influence was just wasted energy and I was determined I wasn't going to waste any more of my valuable resource. Waking up on Monday morning, I was back to Mel who had happily danced and sung along to Bazza without a care in the world.

"We know the working patterns aren't working for any of us or our customers." Looking round the room I could see people nodding their heads in agreement. "So I am proposing we change them," said Robert bravely.

There were some derisive noises, whilst others looked smugly at each other.

"We got it wrong and I'm sorry. We don't want to make another mistake and so this time we'd like to involve you in coming up with ideas. We want you to suggest working patterns you feel might be better for us."

Silence. It was clear the team wasn't expecting Robert to utter those words.

We were back in the emotional roller coaster room, as I had chosen to label it, for round two of negotiations regarding the maintenance team working hours. The team had time to gather their thoughts and then began the onslaught of comments and questions.

"We knew they wouldn't work," stated George, one particularly disgruntled team member. "Well we had to try didn't we," replied Robert quite calmly.

"Why can't we go back to the old hours?"

"Because George, they didn't work either. We need to find a pattern that will work for you, our customers and the business overall."

"Well you're the managers surely it's your job to do this." George was clearly getting in the flow and had elected himself chairperson of the group.

"Well we could. But we got it wrong. So we thought as you are the ones on the front-line you may be able to come up with an idea of how we can work better." Robert's words seemed to land for George and he quietened down.

"Look, I would love it if we could go back to working 8 'til 4 Monday-Friday, but that doesn't work for our customers or the business, so we need to change. We will look at any ideas you come up with as long as they meet customer demand and don't cost us any more money. Are you up for the challenge?"

The team reluctantly agreed.

In the 1960s Elizabeth Kübler-Ross developed a model to explain the grieving process. The focus of her research was terminally ill patients and how they would progress through the different stages of grief when told about their illness.

Since then the *Change Curve* has been widely used as a method for helping us understand our reactions to significant change or upheaval. the different stages we can go through when we are dealing with any sort of change. According to the model there are five stages:

- Grief (comprising shock and/or denial)
- Anger (this may involve finding someone to blame)
- Bargaining (finding ways to postpone the inevitable)
- Depression (feelings of fear, sadness, guilt may pop up here)
- Acceptance (resigning themselves to the situation)

These stages do not always happen in a linear order and people might move on from one stage only to revisit it at a later date. People may also get stuck in certain stages for a long while. Every situation is different, and every person is different, but it is a massively powerful tool in helping individuals and organisations deal with change.

Consider a change that has happened to you. Think back to your feelings when you first found out about it and how your feelings changed over time.

Did you finally reach the acceptance stage or are you currently stuck in one of the other stages?

What would it take for you to move on? Do you want to move on?

Note down any feelings or thoughts you might be having.

For the fish that have opened their hearts and minds to Cod-seerge's service it has been a liberating experience. No longer waiting for someone else to take control of their destiny, they now realise they are able to decide what they do and how they respond to situations. They can move forward with confidence.

Unfortunately, those fish who chose to turn away from Cod-seerge have either remained rooted to the spot, moved down the exp-wrasse elevator or sustained injuries, which will mean they will be out of action for quite a while.

Keen to thank *Noahshark* for his wisdom and guidance, the fish seek him out. However, *Noahshark* doesn't want their gratitude. He is insistent he has done nothing more than introduce Cod-seerge to them. They themselves have done the hard work and consequently as a result of their efforts they are able to move on from the exp-wrasse elevator.

Having proved they are open to change the fish are now able to use the Capelin Cars.

CHAPTER TEN

THE CAPELIN CARS

Communication.

In every business I have ever been in or worked with, there has always been a need to improve communication. No matter what the perceived problem, it is always in the mix. Both as an element of the challenge and the possible solution.

And in all this time there has only ever been one enlightened person who said "Mel, we don't need any more communication, there is already far too much. We just need to get better at it."

This wonderful statement came from a front-line supervisor who was fed up with the barrage of emails he received on a daily basis and the meetings he was asked to attend. In his words, "It never achieves very much and takes me away from my team and my customers."

The problem with communication very rarely relates to volume or frequency. The challenge lies in what is being said and how it is being delivered.

Ellie, my eldest daughter is a cool communicator.

Whether it is on text or face to face she always starts with "Mum." Nothing more, nothing less. No, "Whatcha," no jumping straight in unannounced, no "Yo mother, how's it hanging?" Just a simple "Mum."

Already my interest is piqued, "Yes?"

"Nellie and Ella are going into town tomorrow."

"Are they?"

"Yes, and I was wondering if I could go too. I have done all my homework." Clever, pre-empting my very first question.

"I suppose so," I respond, knowing there is more to come. At this point I realise I am scuppered because she has already got me into a *yes* mindset.

"They're going to see *Mamma Mia 2* at the cinema and you loved it, didn't you?" Ellie knew the answer before she asked the question. Whether intentionally or not she was setting me up to become one of those nodding dogs.

"Yes, I did, I thought it was fab."

"Well I would love to go and find out for myself."

"Would you?"

"Yes, so I am wondering if I can have some money. Please, I love you, you're the best mum ever."

Slam dunk!

Ellie has it in the bag. The words of endearment are merely the thick crumble topping laid carefully over my stewed apples.

Of course, I give her money. Her success rate using this approach is about 99.6%. The other 0.4% is usually when my inner critic is tormenting me and I can't get guacamole out of my hair. On these occasions my stock

answer to any question is "NO, go away, leave me alone, I want to be miserable."

We often label *poor communication* as an organisational weakness, but is it really? We communicate on either a one-to-one or one-to-many basis so how can responsibility fall to the organisation rather than the individual?

Communication is where individuals have the most power to influence what happens. Of course, there may be company guidelines about some forms of communication, but for the most part when we go into work we choose how we communicate.

And we don't always do a great job because when we communicate, we mostly think about ourselves not the person receiving our message.

The all staff email announcing a university's restructure programme was a great example of this. The objective was to inform every member of university staff—so the quickest and easiest way to do this was via email. Had they thought about how the email was going to be received?

Possibly, from the point of view of the general reaction of the masses. But from the perspective of you and I and what we would have personally been feeling, most definitely not. If they had, they never would have sent it in the first place.

And this is one of the reasons why we struggle with communication. We think about what we want to say, not the response we will get.

Had Ellie chosen only to consider her needs and not my response, she may have decided to adopt the typical teenage approach of "Mum, I am going into town tomorrow and need £10 to go to the cinema."

My response would have been "NO, NO, NO!"

Ellie always was and still is a very smart cookie.

Your fellow fish are on the move. Using the Capelin Cars, they are now able to move from tree to tree. Of course, there are still a number of fish who are refusing to embrace change and are therefore stuck where they are, but you understand only they can make the choice about whether or not they move on.

So far, you've only taken a short ride on the capelin car to move higher up the tree. The views are amazing and for the first time you are clearly able to see the lake, it is no longer just a vision, but something tangible. You can't yet touch it, but you are getting closer. Interestingly, as you take in what you can see from this new vantage point you realise you can no longer see the ground as clearly as you once did.

We are all different and how we react to the communication we receive is different. It's why when we ask two colleagues for some information, we may get what we need the very same day from one person and still be chasing the other a week later because they interpreted our request as non-urgent.

The world of communication is a complex game, like the Rubik's Cube, chess and pheasant all rolled into one. How we choose to communicate is driven by the part of our behavioural iceberg we cannot see. How the message is received depends on the recipient. And their reaction is influenced by their own iceberg. Consequently, we may not get the response we expect.

With such a confusing and complicated game, perhaps the best approach would be to lock ourselves in a McDonald's stockroom and gorge ourselves on burgers. And chips. Whilst stacks of avocados stand guard to ensure not even the sneakiest of inner critics can get through to us.

Unfortunately, much as we may wish to do this, it isn't a viable option, so the only solution is to do the best we can, becoming hyper aware of our behaviour and the behaviour of those we communicate with.

"For the last few years," I was standing on stage giving my first speech as director to the hundreds of people in my department, "it's been tough working in an environment where we don't know if our jobs our safe. Sometimes the not knowing is far worse than having a definitive answer, even if it isn't the news we want to hear."

The team had already heard how brilliant they all were and I had set out my vision for the future, but now the time had come to address the walrus in the room.

For a number of years, the team had worked under the threat of restructure and redundancy. Chinese Whispers were a daily occurrence and the dramas which played out as a result of the team's fear and demotivation fuelled the blame culture and silo mentality. It was an issue that needed to be addressed.

It would have been easy to ignore the cinnamon coloured marine mammal with large tusks, by throwing a gigantic carpet over it and just focusing on the good stuff. But that would have been cowardly and in direct conflict with my core values of honesty and building quality relationships. Instead I chose to address the issue head on.

"I can confirm there is going to be a restructure, but it is not being driven by cost savings. Currently, as a department, we are very hierarchical. This hinders our decision-making and means we are not always delivering the best service we can." Looking out into the audience I could see there were some nodding heads. There were also some death stares.

Gulping slightly, I continued, knowing my inner critic was googling *Death Stares for Dummies*.

"I know this is not the news you wanted to hear but sometimes we have to make tough decisions and I wanted to be honest with you. Life isn't always fair, and I wish there was another way but there isn't. I promise we are going to make this process completely transparent and we are also going to support everyone through it."

It was the toughest speech of my career and the most critical. How would the team have felt if they had listened to a wonderfully positive and motivating speech and then just a few weeks later been told the department was going through a reorganisation.

They would have known I had been aware of the changes at the time of the speech and I had chosen not to share my knowledge. In one fell swoop I would have lost their trust and respect. They deserved better. So I chose truth and honesty.

When have you felt cheated, annoyed or frustrated by someone else's communication or behaviour?

Although you are no longer able to see the ground as you once did, you are very appreciative of the capelin cars because they have provided you with the ability to view situations from different perspectives. No longer firmly entrenched in your version of reality, you are starting to develop flexibility and understand that the other fish may not view the world the way you do.

Having taken a ride to the top of the tree you are now going to be brave and use the capelin cars to transport you to another tree. It's scary because you cannot quite believe such a contraption will keep you safe when you are suspended mid-air with nothing between you and the ground.

The capelin car is slowly making its way towards you. Looking down, you realise how high up you are, and feel apprehensive. Breathing rapidly, feeling your heart banging against your chest, you tell yourself you can do this. You have given yourself permission to change, so now is the time to grab the opportunity and move on.

The capelin car arrives at your stop and slowly opens its doors. Taking a deep breath and closing your eyes just for a moment you move forward into the capsule and the doors close. A little jolt and you're off. As you begin to trust the capelin car will not let you down, you relax and start to enjoy the ride, relishing the beauty that is all around you.

The multitude of colours on the leaves of the trees, the graceful movement of your fellow fish and the blue of the sky with clouds that look like balls of cotton wool. Life is good and a far cry from the desolate existence you had whilst you were in the toxic river. You cannot wait to get to your next destination.

On the occasions when you have had to deliver bad news or give someone some constructive feedback, what happened?

Most of us would prefer to bury ourselves in blancmange and pretend life is all sparkly like a rainbow unicorn than deal with these situations. And if that isn't possible, we will resort to hiding behind a process and using any communication tool which will ensure we are not physically present when the recipients receive the bad news.

Despite what we may tell ourselves, it's not because we are worried about the person receiving the information. We are focusing on our feelings and our emotions.

Giving someone bad news is horrible. It can be uncomfortable and we can be fearful the recipient will shoot the messenger. Should that stop us from being fearless, rocking up and delivering the news face to face? Absolutely not.

As decent human beings we should want to be there. To help the recipient process what they have just heard. This may come in the form of some comforting words, a heartfelt touch or even silence. For the person who has received the news just knowing there is someone else in the room may be enough.

Restructures are tough.

They are distressing for the people who may be impacted by the changes but also for those who have to oversee and manage the process. If you have ever been responsible for one you will have been told to consider the roles not the people. This is a great concept in theory but applying it in reality is much harder to achieve.

There was a knock at my pink door, "Can I have a word, Mel?"

"Of course, Richard, come into my office." Richard was our head gardener and had been with the maintenance team for twelve years.

Whilst we were reviewing the structure of the department, my senior management team and I concluded we no longer needed the role of head gardener. Created a few years previously, it was a senior role with responsibility for establishing and implementing a grounds' strategy for our large and ecologically diverse campus.

At the time, Richard had been a fantastic senior gardener and been promoted into the role. While the desire to have a senior position responsible for strategy had been admirable, the reality was, with our limited resources what we actually needed was more gardeners out and about doing the day-to-day work. With such a large campus the grounds team were struggling with the basic upkeep of the site.

Richard was a thoroughly lovely man. With curly blonde hair and a smile that could light up Wembley Stadium even when England was losing 2:1 to Germany in the final of the European Football Championships and the beer had run out. Everybody loved Richard.

Deciding to put his role at risk was just awful: the hardest decision of the entire reorganisation project. However much we all liked Richard as a person, from a business perspective we knew we were doing the right thing. The role of head gardener was no longer needed.

Admitting we are finding things tough is hard isn't it? Often people believe it's a sign of weakness but it's not. It's a sign of strength.

"Really, I'm not sure about that?" Oh no she's back, my inner critic. I must have depressed the mute button by mistake.

"Hello, my dear friend."

"Do you really want people knowing your weaknesses? Would you like to admit to eating all the chocolate eggs you'd bought your children for Easter because you were finding it tough, because, of course, calorie-controlled diets are tough, they're calorie-controlled."

"Uh no. But I did go out and buy some more eggs to replace them."

"Or the time you pretended to your partner you had no clue where his favourite shirt had gone? You tried to convince him he had left it while on holiday when really you had burnt it *"by mistake"* and I am doing the air bunnies there by the way, when you were ironing."

"Oh, snap girl! You're being harsh today."

"You call it harsh, I call it a warm and meaningful friendship," replies my inner critic self-righteously.

"Potato, potahto! I am talking about the important stuff. Like admitting you are struggling to cope with the volume of work, you don't know how to approach a new project and you find performance chats with your team uncomfortable and difficult."

And with that I once again hit the mute button and for added security put duct tape over it.

Early on in my career I struggled with performance chats. I had no issues letting people know how amazingly awesome they were, but talking about areas for improvement brought me out in hives. I would stress about it for days, have sleepless nights and dread it as much as if a group of pirates demanded I walk the plank, whilst balancing a bowl of blancmange on my head and talking nicely to my inner critic.

Once I was sat in the room with the person concerned my hands would shake, I would start talking in vocal fry and often my words would get jumbled up. The person in the room with me must have wondered what was going on and whether the real Mel had been abducted by aliens and replaced by a pretty useless pod person.

When have you had a similar experience?

One where you have got yourself into such a kimchi about a situation, when you come to deal with it, the true version of you has all but disappeared and been replaced by a second-rate imposter.

"I don't want to leave the university. I like the work, I like the people. Is there any way I can stay?" Richard asked, pleading and wringing his hands. He spoke with such softness it was impossible not to catch the sadness in his voice.

His voice cracked. Something shattered inside him and suddenly I was standing in the broken shards of Richard. The smile was replaced by a contorted jagged scar, but even then he was trying to lift the corners.

Completely despondent, the air began to leave my body and my shoulders started to droop. Totally deflated I bowed my head in shame. Eventually, taking a deep breath, I looked up, and said with all the control I could muster, "I don't think so. I am really sorry, but we just don't need the role of head gardener."

"I know you don't," Richard replied gently. There was a painful silence.

"Could I take one of the new posts?"

A slight pause. A massive influx of air. No longer despondent and deflated, I am an inflatable lady, flying without wings, high in the sky with Westlife. "Of course, you could," I replied. All the while thinking why would Richard want to do that? It was two grades lower than his current role and he would no longer be solely responsible for the team.

"Really? That's fantastic," said Richard, beaming from ear to ear. England had just equalised in the final few seconds of extra time.

"Yes, but you do know you would have to take a salary cut after a certain period of time?"

"I don't care. I love it here and I don't want to leave." And with that Richard strode across the room, picked me up and swung me around like I was a little doll. When he put me down he was crying and never having been one to let people cry alone, I began crying as well.

So many tears. Richard's, because he was able to stay at the university. Mine, because I did not have to let a thoroughly lovely man leave the University of Studymore. It was a humbling moment, filled with great learning.

With the definition of insanity ringing in my ears I knew it was crazy to keep having the same performance chats. Getting into a piccalilli beforehand, allowing a pretty mediocre pod person to do my job for me and leaving the person on the receiving end wondering what on earth was going on. Something had to change. I turned to a trusted colleague to ask her advice.

Veronica had years of management experience behind her and was well respected by her team, her colleagues, her peers. Over a steaming cup of decadent hot chocolate complete with whipped cream and marshmallows and sprinkles. And a flake. I needed the sugar fix to give me the courage to admit what was troubling me. I explained what had been going on.

"We've all been there at some point in our career," Veronica replied. "I'm not sure anyone wakes up in the morning and thinks, 'Great, I've got three performance chats today, life could not be better.'"

I laughed. Veronica always had a straight-talking, down-to-earth, tell-it-like-it-is manner. Like inner critic but a decent, well-rounded human being.

"Thank goodness for that, I thought it was just me. But what can I do about it?"

"That's easy," Veronica said, wide-eyed. "When you walk into the room, you sit down, look the person in the eye and tell them how you are feeling. You don't rehearse what you are going to say, you just let whatever is bubbling up inside you come out as words. Be genuine and honest and let it come from the heart." As Veronica said this, she gently touched my arm and I noticed her beautifully painted crimson red nails.

"And that's it, you don't have any other words of wisdom for me?" I asked, slightly bemused.

"No, that's it," replied Veronica joyfully. "Let me know how you get on."

As I picked up my hot chocolate, I wished more than anything it contained a couple of shots of brandy. Smiling bravely at Veronica I secretly wondered if she had been taking helpfulness lessons from my inner critic.

Without even knowing it, Richard taught me a valuable lesson I have never forgotten. When he walked into my office and asked for help to ensure he could stay at the university I initially rebuffed his request because I did not believe there was a solution.

There was of course. But I didn't see it. Not because I didn't want to, but because I was looking at the world through my eyes, not Richard's. Using my own values as a barometer I had decided Richard would never consider taking a job two grades lower than his current role.

A decision I made based on what was important to me. At no point did I consider Richard would have a different view and make a different decision.

"I'm going to be honest with you," I was sat in my office talking to Sarah, one of my colleagues, who I had worked with for over three years. You could not get a more hard-working and committed individual. "I'm not feeling at all comfortable with this. I know you do a fantastic job, but I've had a complaint and I need to have a chat with you about it."

"No worries, I bet it was from Jo in Accounts."

And it was as simple as that. Taking Veronica's advice, I decided to give the honest approach a try the next time I had a performance chat. Unbelievably, it worked! It also worked with the next chat and the one after that.

By choosing not to do what I had always done, I changed the outcome. No longer did performance chats cause me the days of worry they once had. And once I started to relax, I found people were much more receptive to my feedback.

Behaviour breeds behaviour.

So, I dare you. Next time you are finding something challenging and you want to hide behind email or a process, don't. Step out of that bowl of pink stuff you have buried yourself in, clean yourself up, cast aside the rainbow unicorn fantasy and go and speak directly to the person/people concerned.

And if you find yourself getting into a bit of a tizz, then be honest with the people about what is going on for you. People won't view it as a sign of weakness, they will admire your bravery and love you all the more for it. If you speak with honesty, then the chances are people will reciprocate with the same gift.

Honest, face-to-face conversations are one sure-fire way to improve our communication.

Find **The Capelin Cars** *in the set of scales to help you plan for your next challenging conversation.*

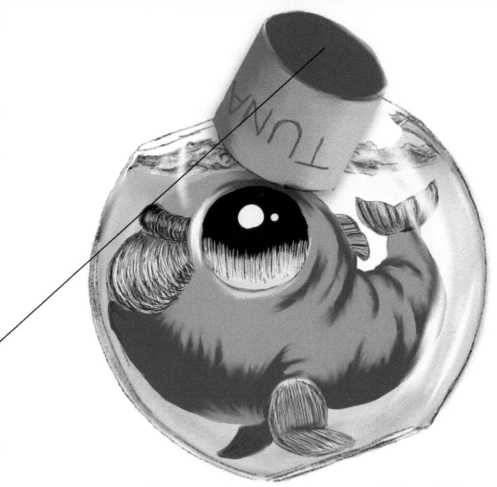

You have arrived at your new destination and are so proud of yourself for being brave and taking the initiative to make positive changes to your life. It's a wonderful feeling but there is one slight niggle. You are no longer able to communicate as effectively with the fish who are still back in the other tree or situated in other parts of your new tree.

Whilst you are moving on, you are keen to ensure you don't lose touch with your fellow fish. Stumped, you wonder what you can do. Memos are too cumbersome and slow. Whilst digital technology is quicker and a more convenient tool to communicate with your fellow fish, you know it can also be impersonal and misinterpreted. You need something else, but what?

And then it comes to you with a flash of your fin. You need a Genuine Porpoise.

CHAPTER ELEVEN

GENUINE PORPOISE

"We cannot not communicate."

Paul Watzlawick

Our communication is not just what we write or what we say.

Think about the times you've walked into a room full of silent people and sensed something is wrong, or you've got home to find your partner grinning from ear to ear and you just know they have got the promotion they were after.

It's because we cannot not communicate. Every behaviour is a form of communication. A hand gesture, a facial expression, an eye movement, all are forms of communication. The majority of our communication is non-verbal.

Yet when businesses are recruiting new people the requirement is always for them to have excellent verbal and written communication skills. I am yet to see a job description that asks for even a basic understanding of non-verbal communication.

Given this slightly bizarre situation, is it any wonder then, that in business, no matter what the issue, communication always forms part of the problem *and* the solution?

It's scary the first time you use the Genuine Porpoise. Focusing on your eyes, body, scale and fins to communicate with your fellow fish rather than the spoken or written word is extremely uncomfortable, but you know they will be portraying the truth about what you are thinking and feeling.

In spite of understanding that this shift will help you communicate better, you have no idea how the other fish will react. You wouldn't be surprised if they turn their backs on you and swim away. If you're honest with yourself, that's what you are expecting to happen.

The research regarding how much of communication is non-verbal ranges from anything upwards of 60% to as much as 93%.

The day a facilitator shared this fact with me, I fell off the chair onto my back and started waving my arms and legs around like I was once again a baby, wishing my parents had shared this information with me when I was a tiny walrus.

It would have saved me years of angst. Instead of worrying about the *exact* words in a presentation I could have spent my time focusing on how I was feeling so that when I was standing on stage I did not have vocal fry like Ursula from The *Little Mermaid* or some other American drag queen.

Nor did I need to hide behind the lectern, holding on for dear life, in case I decided to do an impromptu impression of a Fosse-choreographed tube man.

When you are preparing for a big meeting, an interview, a presentation, where do you focus your attention?

Do you spend hours researching the facts you want to quote, the message you want to relay, the words you want to use?

Yes, of course you do.

And how long do you spend focusing on how you are feeling, and the non-verbal elements of your communication?

Not very long, if any time at all. We might take one or two deep breaths before we enter a room or begin speaking, but not much more than that.

If we want to get better at this communication game; if we want to get more of the jobs we go for, if we want to nail a presentation or meeting, then we need to pay more attention to our non-verbal communication.

And in order to improve our non-verbal communication, we need to become aware of our bodies and how we are feeling. The easiest and simplest way to do this is to start to pay attention to our breathing. Our breath is a fantastic reflection of how we are feeling and yet how often do we pay it any intention.

Let's think about this for a moment.

When you are calm and relaxed, how are you breathing?

Is it slow and even? You may not even notice you are breathing.

What about when you've been doing some fairly active exercise?

Is your breathing faster and louder? You may be breathing through your mouth.

And how about when you're angry and annoyed?

It may be faster still, raspier and if you're apoplectic with rage it could even be, you're struggling for breath.

Different emotional states, different breathing. If you want to alter your state, alter your breathing.

Close to three-quarters of the world's population, including much of the developing world, now has access to a mobile phone. We love our phones. We can't imagine life without them. But some of us may still be able to remember a world when a phone was merely a device that plugged into the wall.

A solid object that used to leave indentations in our fingers as we pulled the dial round to add numbers, had the choice of only one preset ringtone and no facility to send a text, leave a message or use as a mirror to check how gorgeous we were looking.

The phones we have today are great. They mean we never need to be out of touch with our family or friends. And at the touch of a button we can see tomorrow's weather, find our way to a new restaurant and

discover the strange noises we make during the night whilst we are sleeping. What a phenomenal piece of technology.

We were on the seventy-second floor of the tallest building in Europe, looking out at the most amazing view of the city of London. It was the thirtieth of June, 2018, and my birthday. The sun was shining and the sky was a brilliant blue. We could not have chosen a better day to visit *The Shard*.

As we stepped out of the lift onto the viewing gallery we felt slightly uneasy on our feet: as though we'd already had too much to drink. "You're fine," advised one of The Shard's guest relations team. "What you are experiencing is perfectly normal. Being so high up the building does move by as much as 10cm." What a comforting thought!

It was truly stunning to be able to see the whole of London. People were busy taking photos and selfies. To celebrate such an important day we decided to treat ourselves to a glass of champagne and, just as if the gods were on our side, two seats became available in the small seating area.

Plonking ourselves down, grateful for the rest, we began people watching, one of our favourite pastimes. There were folk from all over the world as well as home-grown nationals like us. Some people were stood still just enjoying the moment whilst others were pointing to various landmarks, keen to show off their knowledge of this wonderful city.

"Oh, look there's the Gherkin and over there is the Walkie Talkie," and then a little more quietly, "that's the Butt Plug," followed by some raucous laughter.

I took a sip of my ice-cold champagne and a couple of the bubbles went up my nose. Giggling, I looked around to see if anyone had noticed (my parents would not have been impressed by my lack of etiquette!). Luckily no one had because, guess what, every single person around us had their heads bent over their phone.

I was astonished.

These people were in one of the most iconic buildings in the world, 72 floors up on a glorious summer's day and their phone screen was more important than enjoying this incredible moment. If those people were a reflection of how the entire world is going to end up, then I want to learn how to time travel. To go back to the world of memos and phones attached to the wall and life without social media.

I want to go back to an era when people had no choice but to be fully present, to enjoy whatever it was they were doing rather than creating more content for social media companies to profit from. I want to return to a time when I wasn't speaking to the top of someone's head. When I was talking to them face to face and making genuine eye contact.

Because if we want to improve our communication, especially our non-verbal communication we need to turn up and be fully present in whatever situation we may find ourselves in. If we aren't, how can we recognise what is going on in our bodies and more importantly how can we notice the non-verbal cues we are getting from the people we are with?

The reaction of your fellow fish to your genuine porpoise is quite amazing. Instead of turning away from you, they respond with their own genuine porpoise and you realise they are reciprocating your honesty. The words each of you are using are still important, but paying attention to your non-verbal communication is much more powerful. How amazing!

Performing a turtle rap, you congratulate yourself on becoming a better communicator.

Print out The Genuine Porpoise *in the set of scales and put it up somewhere in your workplace as a constant reminder of some of the non-verbal cues you should pay attention to.*

It's Wednesday morning, 9.30am [best Newcastle commentator voice], and at the IT company the sales team and developers are sat in a conference room for their regular monthly meeting. Only five minutes into the conversation the drama begins.

"You're not listening to me! We had this conversation last month," says Stan. Clearly for him the memory of being locked in a box of spiders, critters and cockroaches still lingers on.

"Yes, I am! You're not listening to me! The client has changed her mind and we need to deliver what she wants," says Ella, her voice rising to match the frustration she clearly feels. It's unclear whether the turkey testicles she is currently eating are adding to her frustration or providing her with the impetus to get what she wants.

Doing my best to stay present and engaged… I was finding it difficult. Having experienced several of these meetings the drama which was unfolding like a reality TV show had become predictable and just a tad boring. Two different people, two different perspectives. Both entrenched in their reality of the world and not willing to listen to any view that wasn't their own.

Ella, the Sales Manager and Stan, the tech guru, always ended up gunning for each other, only ever affording each other the luxury of listening so they could reply and hammer home their opinion.

Would you say you were a good listener? On a scale of one to ten, where ten is a Townsend's big-eared bat and one is a glucose-filled toddler, how good a listener are you?

Many of us may think we have fabulous listening skills, when in reality we are just one Haribo away from pretend aeroplanes and scrawling demon-like Pokémon on the walls.

Listening to someone is actually much harder than many of us may think. In order to *actively* listen we need to rock up, be fully present and

suspend our own judgement or preconceived ideas. And when we hear something that jars with us, or we spot moss in somebody's beard, we mustn't fixate but keep listening without interruption.

Brené Brown, a research professor from the University of Houston, believes when we hear something we don't agree with, we shouldn't jump in and respond, we should keep listening. Keep listening until we truly understand what the other person is saying.

How many of us really do that?

With my clients, I can absolutely say with 100% certainty I actively listen to what they are saying. I may interject with questions to help me understand what is going on for them but there is no interrupting to respond. With my friends, my family, my daughters, well I may try but often I fail.

"Isn't that the truth! How about properly listening to me once in a while?"

Good grief, how much licking does it take to unstick duct tape? "Did you say something?"

"RUDE!"

Using the genuine porpoise at every opportunity has definitely improved your communication with your fellow fish, especially on a one-to-one basis.

You are becoming much more curious about non-verbal cues. No longer are you choosing to go with standard prejudgements around fish behaviour; assuming that just because a fish has crossed its fins, it is getting defensive. But rather, you are taking your time to gather in all the different non-verbal cues to better understand what might be going on.

In addition, by listening actively to what your fellow fish are saying you are able to better comprehend their perspective. You no longer rush in to speak over them or prove your point. You take time to process what they are saying and base your response on what you have heard.

You thought you had nailed *communication* with the genuine porpoise, but you now realise it signified the beginning of the journey not the end. Consequently, it's time to take all your learnings and self-awareness and create an even more sophisticated method of communication that will allow you to communicate with many fish at once.

The Fin-to-net.

CHAPTER TWELVE

THE FIN-TO-NET

You've met my inner critic. She's difficult and surly and only ever comes to say hello when I am finding things tough or there is an opportunity to put me down in some way.

"That is just not true, I am your BFF, your one and only BFF if truth be told!"

See what I mean?

When was the last time you had a conversation with your inner critic?

You know, that voice in your head that loves to remind you how disgusting, worthless, hideous and insignificant you are. The one that can stop you from doing all those amazing, wonderful things you would like to do.

I am yet to meet someone who doesn't have an inner critic. For some, the inner critic can really hold them back from being the best version of themselves. For others, they may have learnt to communicate effectively with theirs. So whilst it might regularly pop up to say hello, they have strategies to ensure it doesn't interfere in the life they want to lead.

The Fin-to-net is working. As an overall communication tool, it has helped you hone your skills even further. The fin-to-net brings together all the different elements of communication; the capelin cars, the genuine porpoise and finguistics. You are now able to communicate as effectively with many fish as you were on a one-to-one basis.

It's a wonderful development and for your fellow fish, it no longer feels like you are merely passing on information, but truly engaging in meaningful conversation.

As a result, you and your fellow fish are much happier. You don't always agree and in fact now there appear to be many more times when there is a difference of opinion. But because you are all comfortable saying what you really feel about a situation honest dialogue is happening on a daily basis.

Our inner critic is born out of the attachments we make to our experiences and the fishnets we have about ourselves. Fishnets are beliefs that can hold us back and limit us. Those elements which sit in the part of our iceberg we cannot see. Sometimes, it's easy to identify what they might be. Other times it is far more difficult.

Examples of fishnets might be: I am not good enough, I can't be myself, there is no hope, I can't do that. The list is endless and will be different for each of us. The impact though will be the same. Fishnets hold us back and can stop us from being truly amazing.

What are your fishnets?

There will be some that easily come to mind, but others may take time to appear. Don't force it, just set the intention that you want to become aware of what they are and over a period of time they will pop, probably when you least expect it.

As you realise what they are write them down on The Fishnets _that you can find in your set of scales._

Understanding our fishnets is extremely powerful. Armed with this knowledge we can make changes, rather than flailing around on the ground being battered by our inner critic.

Saying goodbye to our fishnets is no easy task, in fact for many of us it becomes a lifelong challenge. We think we've nailed it and then something pops up in our life that we weren't expecting and they are back again.

There are lots of strategies that can be used to diminish the power of our inner critic and the fishnets they use: reading around the subject, chatting to fellow sufferers or finding yourself a coach. If none of these work, you could always adopt my particular favourites—the avocado threat, mute button or duct tape, depending what end they are talking out of.

You can also choose how you communicate with your inner critic. Some people choose to compassionately embrace their inner critic, thanking it for coming to say hello, acknowledging it only has their best interest at heart and then very politely moving it to one side, so they can make a more rational decision.

For others, treating it like they are in a boxing match with Mike Tyson is the way they choose to engage with their inner critic. Whenever they feel a punch coming their way they move to avoid it and hit back ten times harder.

Neither is right or wrong and the approach that is right for you may not be right for me. It may also be that on some occasions when life is going well we want to take on Mike, but when life is a little bit harder we choose the slightly softer approach.

For me, I have a warrior to help me battle against my inner critic. Let me introduce you to my alter ego, Mel B.

Yes, for those of you who do know of The Spice Girls, my alter ego was a creation inspired by this 1990s pop group and most especially Scary Spice.

"I hate Mel B. She is mouthy and scary, and she definitely won't listen to me," says my inner critic petulantly, folding her arms and scowling like a spoilt brat. "She talks out of her zig-a-zig-ah!"

"Yes, you are absolutely right. And she's exactly what I need to ensure I don't let you ruin my life."

Mel B is the brave version of me and has a unique accent which is far more home counties meets Brummie mummy than Leeds. She is quite happy to step out of her comfort zone, not frightened of failure and sees life as an adventure where no opportunity should ever be passed up.

Mel B is the one who stands up to my inner critic and says thanks for your thoughts, but your opinion is most definitely not required.

Mel B was the person who told me I could ride the *Pepsi Max Big One* in Blackpool (when I have an abject fear of roller coasters), sing karaoke in a packed bar (even though I had been on orange juice all night) and write a book, this book.

In spite of the fin-to-net, there is still one hook in your fishbowl. And no matter how your communication skills have improved, you have still not discovered the best way to deal with it. This hook can be so awful to you and say the most abhorrent things. It has you doubting your own abilities and would, if it could, take you back to the toxic river and ensure you stay there forever.

Sometimes you feel you are making headway because let's face it you made it out of the toxic river. Through your determination not to give up and willingness to try lots of different modes of transport you were able to firstly make it on to the bank of the river and then up into the tree.

Since then, despite all the cruel messages the hook has been giving you, you have listened to the wise words of *Noahshark* and taken action. You accepted responsibility for your behaviour and expressed a willingness and desire to change so you could use the capelin cars, genuine porpoise and fin-to-net. Amazing and wonderous achievements, but still this spiteful hook has the ability to hold you back.

If we're not careful our inner critic can keep us from experiencing some of life's greatest adventures. It can also affect how we view others and the relationships we have with them.

Most people were scared of my boss Paul. And truth be told many just tolerated him because he was in a position of power. But when you dug underneath the surface you realised it was all a charade. I worked closely with him for fifteen years and I can definitively say he was a good man, although at times his behaviour was truly shocking.

He was a man who never believed he was good enough, but rather than admit those feelings and let anyone see the *true* Paul he preferred to cast himself in the role of the pantomime villain: wicked, argumentative and cantankerous.

And by doing so he was disliked by many within his team and across the university. These feelings fuelled his beliefs and in the end he created a self-fulfilling prophecy.

Paul didn't believe he was good enough, so he behaved in a way that ensured other people didn't think so either, which fuelled his original feelings and ensured the cycle of self-flagellation and self-loathing continued ad infinitum.

It doesn't condone his behaviour and it certainly doesn't excuse it, but it does provide some context and understanding if you wanted to be gracious and chose to look beyond the surface.

This behavioural enigma is complex and confusing and it's no wonder we get ourselves in a gherkin, cheese-grater or other food-related tower about it, especially at work. However, if we want to start to get to grips with this, we need to make changes at a personal level.

The very first step is accepting who we are and loving ourself no matter what. There is not a single solitary person on this planet who is perfect. And for those of us, like Kate, who have tried to take accountability for perfection, we know it is a thoroughly exhausting and completely unachievable exercise.

We are all perfectly imperfect and once we accept this life can become a lot easier.

Karin and I met at university. It was day one and I was stood in a faceless corridor, looking intently at a dark green noticeboard hoping it would magically tell me where I needed to be. I was desperately trying to put on a brave face as I didn't know a single other person.

"Are you on the hospitality course?" a warm voice, with just the hint of a Scandinavian accent, asked.

I gratefully turned around to see a short blonde girl with a lopsided grin and intelligent brown eyes standing behind me, looking as confused as I was.

And in that single second a friendship was struck that would last a lifetime. Enjoying moments of wonder, pregnancy, birth, love, marriage, and weathering the storms, marital breakup, moving home, relocating to a new country, redundancy and the loss of loved ones. Whether it was life's highs or lows there would always be love, laughter and vodka.

Two very different people, we just connected. Karin was recently married and living in a hotel in central London. University was just one part of Karin's very busy life, whereas for me it was the absolute focus of my attention. As laid-back and relaxed as Karin was, I was frantic and uptight.

My assignments were always complete and ready way before the deadline date whereas Karin frequently pulled all-nighters to ensure she got the work in on time. I pushed myself to get the best grades whilst Karin was just happy to go with the flow and get whatever grade she was awarded. Fortunately, she was a very bright individual so good marks came naturally to her.

Four years passed in a whirlwind of good times, hysterical hilarity and a tiny touch of alcohol. In June 1993 we sat our finals. Karin was

pregnant and not just a little bit pregnant. She was eight months pregnant and gave birth just three weeks later to baby Emma. Beautiful Emma who became my goddaughter.

As Karin was getting to grips with breast feeding and adjusting to life as a mother, I was busy looking for a job, which wasn't easy. One day as we sat on the soft and squidgy cream sofa which filled her lounge, surrounded by baby paraphernalia (nappies, wipes, changing mat, soft toys), Karin decided it was time to share some of her wisdom with me.

"Mel, you know I love you, but you push yourself so hard. You expect so much of yourself and you're going to be so disappointed by people who don't do the same."

I looked at her, unsure what she really meant and said "Thanks, I know." But I didn't.

I had no clue what she meant, and it would take me years to understand how profound her insight was.

It's exhausting. Going up against the hook in your bowl, saps your energy. In spite of all your new-found communication skills, you have not yet found the formula to ensure the hook no longer holds you back from becoming the remarkable fish you want to be.

All this time, it has felt like a war. A war of wills. Occasionally you will win a battle but more often than not it is the hook who is victorious. Perhaps you need to try a different approach. One where there is no force, no fighting.

A Tang glider would enable you to do this. A Tang glider that allows you to soar above the tops of the tree. On the Tang glider no hooks are allowed and so you will have no choice but to leave it behind!

CHAPTER THIRTEEN

THE TANG GLIDER

Family.

We all have one. It may not be the traditional definition of a mum, dad and two kids, but we all have a family of sorts.

We love them, we hate them. We are their biggest fans and their biggest critics. The pendulum of emotion we have for these people can swing from minute to minute, day to day, year to year, but the fact remains, they will always be our family. No matter what. They are typically the people we turn to and rely on when the going gets tough.

How many times have you been on a training course, had a really good time, could see merit in the subject matter but when you got back to your desk, you didn't do anything differently? Well maybe you did but only for a short while and then you went back to your old habits.

Organisations often believe that training is the key to creating sustainable change, but it isn't.

Freedom.

The Tang glider has created a feeling of freedom like nothing you have ever experienced before. Flying high above the trees you savour the lightness you feel, having removed the shackles that horrible and vindictive hook had attached to you.

Now you are finally free, you are able to see the endless possibilities. You can choose to do anything you want, be anyone you want. The sense of liberation is truly exhilarating.

For the moment though you just want to enjoy the here and now. As a *flying fish* you marvel at the airstreams which are enabling you to soar through the sky. Looking around, you once again see your lake and know you are getting even closer to it.

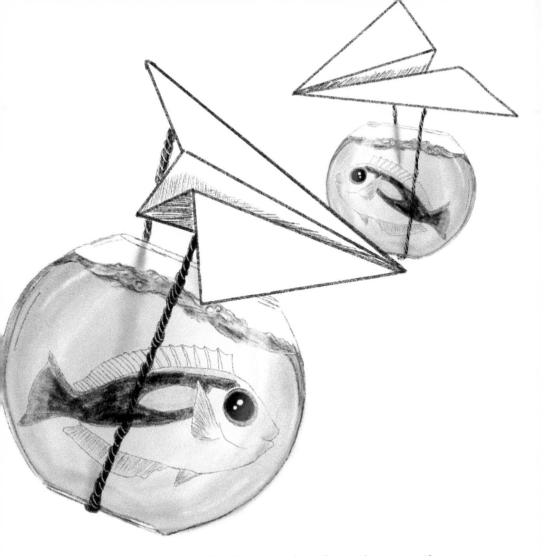

Every weekday morning, the alarm sounds and my tube-man self jumps straight out of bed, Fosse dancing my way into the bathroom. Once there, I shower and clean my teeth until I get that sparkly glint, knowing people will have to wear sunglasses to protect themselves from my dazzling smile.

And using my electric toothbrush, which amazingly revived itself after dying at the cleverness of Sigmund Freud, I always clean my teeth the same way. Bottom front, bottom back, top back, top front. It's exactly the same routine at night, I never have to think about it.

Having showered and cleaned my teeth it's then time to rouse the girls. That's when the routine stops.

They may wake up as angels or devils or even King Kong. Stomping around with sleep-ruffled hair standing on end, scaring the entire inhabitants of the house, the creepy crawlies and the remnants of last night's dinner. Ready to swallow up any other person who says something they don't like, ranging from "Good Morning," to "Your toast is ready," or "Would you like to wear your red shoes to school?"

What is your morning routine? Which activities do you do on autopilot and which actions are a little more fluid?

The conscious competence ladder, helps us understand the different learning phases we go through to adopt a new skill:

Stage 1

Unconsciously Unskilled—*we don't know we don't have this skill or that we need to learn it*

Stage 2

Consciously Unskilled—*we know that we don't have this skill*

Stage 3

Consciously Skilled—*we know that we have this skill*

Stage 4

Unconsciously Skilled—*we don't know that we have this skill (it just seems easy)*

Let's think about cleaning our teeth. As babies we didn't have this skill but hopefully by the time most of us were four or five years old, we had become unconsciously skilled in the art of keeping our teeth clean and stain free.

And for those of us that drive, when we had our very first driving lesson, we had no idea we would need to develop the skill of *mirror, signal, manoeuvre*. When my instructor first asked me to carry out the move, sat in his little red Ford Fiesta, I didn't think I would ever get the hang of this uncomfortable three-stage movement.

"Mirror, signal, manoeuvre," I kept saying to myself. "Mirror, signal, manoeuvre." And then one day I no longer had to say it, the action had become a habit, so much so I didn't even realise I was doing it.

If these are the four stages we go through in order to change and acquire new skills, then it's no wonder training isn't as effective as organisations would like it to be. I have never known any organisation consider how they move their people through the different phases of the competency ladder to ensure new skills are completely embedded.

Sat on hard wooden benches in a tiny little theatre in Haketon a group of proud parents were watching their children perform *Alice in Wonderland*. The children had been on a one-day *Play in a Day* workshop and the production was a culmination of their efforts.

Twenty children were on stage tightly holding their scripts, doing their very best to entertain their parents. There were some natural actors amongst them, but many looked uncomfortable and out of place. The majority looked down at their script when reading their lines whilst others spoke so fast the words ran into each other and it was impossible to decipher what they were saying.

As parents, we didn't necessarily see this in our own child because we were awash with pride, but as we watched the other little people we cringed, sensing their unease. Whilst we were willing them all to be amazing thespians the reality was slightly more painful.

Effecting change in an organisation is tough. When we consider the challenges a 30% success rate is in fact an astounding achievement. Firstly, however much an organisation may want to change its people, it can't. The only person who can change you is you. No matter how much your business may hammer home the need for you to change, if you don't want to you won't.

Secondly, if your business wants to have any chance of encouraging you to change, they need to connect with the chunk of your behaviour iceberg they cannot easily see. What may connect for you, may not connect for your colleagues and therefore, however your business chooses to communicate with you it needs to be tailored to your specific needs.

Putting all employees through a standardised training programme will be like dipping sheep. Whilst this may be a very effective method for killing ticks and mites it is not a useful tool in helping businesses change.

Although training is not the answer there is a solution.

The first and absolutely crucial step is that an organisation acknowledges it cannot force its people to change. This change in mindset will cause a shift in behaviour. No longer will it want to use brute force to break down the door to change but gently open it and encourage its people to walk through to the other side.

Julie and I began working together in 2009. She came to the University of Studymore to provide additional temporary cover for the admin team. Short, with dark brown hair and a very professional manner, within just a couple of weeks she had turned my life around.

Julie was quick to learn and incredibly pro-active. Anything I asked her to do was actioned immediately and for the first time ever I had admin support I could 100% rely on. When I handed something over, I knew I could forget about it because it would be actioned and completed on time.

This amazing woman was a real find and I knew she had oodles of potential.

Three days later we were back, sitting on the same uncomfortable benches watching our children's production after another *Play in a Day* workshop. On this occasion there were less than ten children and the focus of the day was improvisation. First thing in the morning the children had been given a black box and were asked to create a play.

The lights went up and we were invited into a world of our children's creativity.

"I'm bored," whines one child.

"Let's play a game," suggests another.

"No. Let's go back to camp and tell each other scary stories."

"Yes!" They all reply.

The opening scene and already the children had us captivated. There were no scripts or rushed words. The children were confident and at ease, inviting us into the world of their imagination. Once back at camp the children found a black box and began telling each other stories about it.

The stage was dark and the soundtrack from *Mission: Impossible* filled the tiny theatre. As the music faded, two MI5 agents dressed in long raincoats and dark glasses fell onto the stage. "Where's the bag?" one asks the other.

"What bag?"

"The bag with black bomb box. Where is it?"

"Oh, I forgot it," replies the other nonchalantly. "I'll just go and get it." She leaves the stage as the other agent begins counting the strands of her beautiful long hair.

"One million and fifty-five, one million and fifty-six."

"I'm back," shouts the agent, re-entering the stage, carrying a brown satchel and holding a coffee mug in her left hand.

"What took you so long?"

"Well I had to get a Starbucks," she says, pointing to the mug, "and ring my mum. Boy can she talk!"

"Well you need to be quiet now," says the agent who has stopped counting her hair. "Because we need to plant this bomb!"

Slowly, taking their guns out, the agents begin moving around the stage looking for any hazards until they stupidly back into each other.

"BOOM!" The bomb explodes and the agents move slowly through the air.

The stage goes dark, amidst the sound of applause and laughter.

The lights go up and there's an old woman on stage talking to her plants. With the aid of a walking stick she deliberately makes her way around. "Since my Burt died," she says, "I've been so lonely and sad. We couldn't have kids, and my sister she well, she lives in Scotland, so I don't get many visitors."

As she talks lovingly to the plants, she notices the black box and gasps. "Why, I haven't seen that box for many years. It's the box where I kept all the letters Burt wrote me during the war. Would you like me to read one to you?"

Hands trembling, the woman opens the box and slowly, carefully, takes out one of the letters. She puts the box down and lovingly smooths out the pages of the letter. A reminiscent smile and she is back in the place and time when she first opened the letter.

Even with her glasses she is struggling to read the words from all those years ago. "My dearest Grace. Life is tough here but the thought of

coming home to you keeps me going despite the cold, the damp and the lack of food. When I come home, we're going to go dancing like we did when we were courting. Have you still got that blue dress, the one you were wearing, when I proposed to you?"

She stops and haltingly looks up. There are tears in her eyes. Slowly she folds the letter back up, unable to read on. "He didn't make it home," she says sadly, to no one in particular. "But I still miss him like it was yesterday." Ever so gently she puts the letter back in the box and closing the lid she lets her hand rest on it as she lets out the most touching sigh.

Once again, the stage goes dark, but this time there is silence. We are all feeling Grace's pain.

And then there is rapturous applause.

For twenty minutes, this small group of children thoroughly entertained us. We caught glimpses of their different personalities and for a short while they invited us into the inner workings of their minds.

"The box is ours!" shouts one group of kids dressed as hillbillies, decked from head to toe in denim, complete with cowboy hats and chequered neckties.

"No, it's not! It's ours!" shouts the other group of mods, in their smart suits and ties.

The two groups charge at each other and skirmishes break out right across the stage. A couple are tousling on the floor, rolling over and over, whilst others are beating each other with sticks. Some are long and thin like spears, whilst others are short and wide and look as though they could inflict real pain.

A number of the group are engaged in martial art style combat, with arms flying out and legs kicking up high.

The noise and energy are overwhelming and it's impossible to know where to look for all the action that is going on. It is unclear which group is winning and will be able to claim the black box as theirs. Eventually the hillbillies win and decide to perform a celebratory haka dance that would have made the New Zealand All Blacks extremely proud.

Feet pounding the floor, arms moving in sync, it's just possible to make out the word *winner* in the sounds they are making.

Towards the end, all the other children join them on stage to finish the dance with pure gusto. As they finish, the audience are on their feet, clapping and whooping and whistling at the children's amazing ability and performance.

It was an absolutely incredible experience and completely different from the one the children had created just a few days previously. It became evident that when the children were given a script and a framework to work within their true spirit and creativity were non-existent.

Create an environment where they were encouraged to use their imagination and had no limits other than the requirement to use a little black box and the results were remarkable.

How different would our workplaces be if we applied this same learning and stopped believing policies and procedures were the panacea to every service failure problem on the planet? That instead of *telling* people what we wanted them to do, we described the outcome we wanted to see and trusted in our team's creativity, experience and imagination to deliver amazing results.

"How are you settling in?" Julie and I are sat in my office planning out the next few weeks in my diary.

"Great, I really love the people here, they are so friendly."

"Yes, we are. We have our moments but we're a pretty good team," I reply, smiling at Julie. "I have to say I have been massively impressed by your work and you have made such a difference to my life, I really can't thank you enough."

"Oh, that's great, thank you," says Julie beaming.

"So, I am just wondering what other amazing talents you have that we could use. What do you enjoy doing?"

"Umm, I've never been asked that before. I probably need to have a think. Is it ok if I come back to you on that?"

"Of course, you can, no worries. We have a one-to-one next week, why don't we catch up then?" Then it's back to diary management.

Babies are the most extraordinary communicators on the planet. Without saying a single word, they have the ability to engage us for hours on end and ensure we do exactly what they want. A toothless smile or a little gurgle will ensure our heart melts and our legs become jelly. So no matter how much work we have piling up around us, we will happily sit and play with them for hours on end.

A howl from the seventh circle of Hades and they will have us running to change their bum, feed them or berate ourselves for getting the two mixed up. We will do whatever it takes to ensure the infernal calling of hell's choir stops, and the quiet, happy bundle of joy is returned to us once more. And as they move on from this stage of absolute helplessness we feel privileged to watch and be part of their development journey.

First, they learn to sit up, crawl, and finally walk. I have been told I missed out on the crawling stage and just used to shuffle along on my bum, like a dog with tapeworm. No doubt this was the starting point for me showing bad manners and why I used to love sticking chips up my nose. You'll be pleased to know this is one unconscious habit I managed to break (at least in public)!

And whilst these wonderful creatures are developing their motor skills, they are also developing their verbal communication, having already become self-declared experts in the art of non-verbal conversation.

As spectators in their journey we *ooh* and *ahh* at their development and for us mums and dads out there, the first time they utter anything that sounds remotely like mummy or daddy, the world fills with the biggest firework display ever.

As adults, we marvel at every stage of these little people's adventure and embrace their creativity and imagination. When they bring us their drawing of a car we don't say, "That's wrong! A car only has four wheels, it's not a centipede," or "You've forgotten the steering wheel, how can you possibly drive a car without it?" or "It's ok, but I wish you had coloured it blue, I had expected the car to be blue."

Instead, we make more weird and wonderful appreciation noises and tell them how bloomin' fantastic they are and we will always love them no matter what. And whilst we are sharing this tender moment with our child we are trying desperately to ignore the fact they are examining what's on their finger, having just stuck it up their nose. Eventually, we can bear it no more and remind them, "It's not polite to pick your nose!"

Sarah is Head of Residences at Caerforclogs University and we have known each other for many years. I always joke she lives in the arse end of nowhere and she tells all her friends I live in London (I don't, and I take as much umbrage at the statement as I do about having a cockney accent). No matter what our views may be about where we live, we do share very similar perspectives about people and their behaviour.

Sarah has a very interesting mindset with regard to her team. She doesn't talk about them as her work colleagues or staff, she calls them her work family. Sarah has her gorgeous family at home and her equally gorgeous family at work.

It helps that she is one of the most engaging and warm people I know. But I wonder what would happen if more of us started to shift our mindset from work colleagues to work family.

When we think about our family members, we think of them as a whole person. We don't think *this is home Alice* and *this is Alice when she's out*. We think of Alice as our sister. Wonderful, gorgeous Alice. The sister who can drive us nuts but who we also love like mad.

How do you view your work colleagues?

Do you think of them as a whole person or are you just interested in their professional side?

Running a management development programme for one of my clients, I knew all the delegates on the course, having worked with them before. As they started to arrive I chatted with each of them about what they had been up to since we'd last seen each other. Stood around the coffee station I glanced at my watch, knowing we would soon need to make start.

At that moment Marios walked in and I thought, "My gosh you seem to have grown taller since I last saw you."

"Sorry, I'm late," he said breathlessly, having clearly run from wherever he had been.

"Don't worry, you're not late," I said smiling. "We've got a few minutes yet. Grab yourself a coffee and take some time." Placing my hand on his arm I gave it a quick rub, wanting to help calm him down.

"Er, Mel, what time are we going to be finishing?"

"It should be around twelve. Is that ok with you or do you need to be somewhere?" I asked curiously.

"No, that should be fine. It's just my daughter gave birth this morning at 3am and I want to go and meet my new granddaughter."

"That's fantastic news, congratulations. Are they both ok?"

"Yes, they're fine," he replied excitedly. "I asked my manager if I could come on this course next week instead, but she said no, although I am taking this afternoon off. The sooner we are done here the quicker I can go and meet baby Eleni."

All credit to Marios, he did do his best to engage during the morning's activities, but it was clear he wasn't really in the room, he was in the hospital with his daughter and granddaughter.

If you were Marios' manager what would have been your response to his request?

Organisations need to understand what happens to someone outside of work will impact their performance in work and vice versa. Consequently, they need to stop believing they can just work with the professional part of their people and start working with the whole person, just as they would do if it was a member of their family.

It won't surprise you to learn that as a toddler Louisa was never content to go out and about in cute kids' clothes. There always had to be a dramatic twist.

Like the time we went out for lunch and she insisted on wearing a pink tutu over her yellow pyjamas. We went shopping and she was in a green princess outfit complete with matching coloured eye shadow and we supported Ellie in her swim competition with Louisa dressed as a Spanish señorita.

Now I could have argued for hours about Louisa's choice of attire or given up and stayed at home but instead I chose to go with the flow and let her be exactly who she was. Needless to say, when we were out and about in public people embraced her individuality and, of course, Louisa loved the attention.

As our children grow, we marvel at how their creativity and imagination feeds their development until one day everything changes.

School.

The first day at school is the moment when things change and our children's creativity and imagination no longer fuels their development in the way it once did.

Our kids need school, but the system has remained virtually unchanged since the Victorian era. However, we are no longer living in Victorian times. We are living in an age where the jobs our children and grandchildren will be doing do not currently exist. An education framework created in the 1800s cannot possibly support these changes.

Teaching methods have evolved. As a school governor I was so pleased to learn our children are no longer expected to sit at a desk all day and write down what the teacher has written on the board like I did. Today children are taught using a myriad of different techniques which tap into their learning styles.

Whatever the rights and wrongs of our schooling system there is no denying it is the point at which creativity and imagination no longer become the driving force for our children's development.

No longer able to wear yellow pyjamas and a pink tutu, Louisa had to wear a school uniform. Ellie was no longer encouraged to be bold and brave, exploring the world in the way she wanted to. Instead it became about learning her sounds, so she could move through different levels of reading books.

Frameworks. Targets. Tests. This is the world our children start to inhabit. Where once it was perfectly acceptable for them to embrace their individuality, now there is a greater steer to fit in and conform. Standing out from the crowd is not something to be applauded. In fact, it can often lead to ridicule and alienation.

And for the next twelve years this is the basis for our children's evolution, as they move forward on their journey towards becoming teenagers and eventually young adults. If we're lucky some of them may hold on to shreds of their imagination and creativity, but for many, conforming to expectations, living within the box, is all they know.

> **To help you consider how your key relationships at work would change if you shifted your mindset to think of them as your work family, find and complete The Tang Glider in your set of scales. I promise you it will be fun!**

"I really hated school. Looking back, I wish I had knuckled down and worked hard, but I didn't." Julie and I were sat in my office discussing her talents and what she liked doing. "When I left school, I had no choice but to go to secretarial college. I wanted to work with my hands and do something creative, but my parents were worried it wasn't a safe job."

"Since then I have spent my whole life in administration. I am a qualified furniture restorer as well because I went to night school part-time and it's something I would like to make a career of in the future. My partner and I have plans to work together as he's a builder, but that won't be for a while yet. Other than that, I don't really know."

Julie didn't know but I sensed this amazingly efficient woman had a lot more potential inside of her and I was determined that together we would find it and unlock it.

We leave the world of education much changed from the child who entered the schooling system aged four or five. Over the course of this time we have waved goodbye to the inventive and enterprising genius inside of us and said hello to the responsible adult we have become.

We enter the workplace being able to work out complex mathematical equations and recite the periodic table. But we have lost some of our innate communication skills, creativity and imagination. We have come to rely much more on our logical brain than our creative brain.

And when we step into this new environment of work the world becomes more confusing still. We are placed back in an environment which wants us to start thinking outside the box again. To generate ideas that will help move our businesses forward.

But to do this we will need to be in a habitat that embraces and encourages creativity and imagination. And not only that, we will need to feel fully supported, so that if we don't get it right first time or an idea fails there is no recrimination or backlash.

Julie went on to achieve great things at the University of Studymore. She became project coordinator for the University's involvement in London 2012 and then a project manager, becoming an integral part of my senior management team when I became director.

During the five years we worked together we became very close. As her biggest supporter I would constantly push her to do things that were out of her comfort zone, but I would also pull her up when I knew she hadn't delivered to the best of her ability.

Meanwhile, Julie would always be there with a comforting word or a chocolate bar when I'd had a tough day, but wouldn't be afraid to tell it to me straight, when she thought I could have handled a situation better.

There was mutual honesty, trust and respect.

Near to the end of my time at Studymore, we were sat on the beanbags in my office just chatting about work and life in general when she piped up and said, "You know what Mel, I wish I had had a teacher like you when I was at school. Someone who had really bothered to take the time to get to know me and find out what I enjoyed."

"But I didn't and until I came here I didn't actually realise you could do jobs you enjoyed. That a job was more than just a means to pay the bills."

For a moment I sat there shocked. Julie's comments had come out of the blue and I hadn't been expecting them. For once, I didn't know how to respond other than to say, "Thank you. That's a really lovely thing to say."

And it was. It was the best gift of feedback I had ever been given.

Having thrown off the restraints the hook had once used to control you, you now have a clarity of thought you never would have believed possible. You need to get to the lake. Once there you know you will be able to find fulfilment. To be happy and enjoy every second of your very existence.

The tang glider has not only enabled you to let go of your own hooks but those hooks you held about your fellow fish. They have become your family and you cannot imagine a life without them. As much as you want to get to the lake you want them to get to there as well and will do whatever you can to support them.

You imagine what it would feel like to be swimming free in the lake's expanse of water. To no longer be separated from your fellow fish by the fishbowls you are in. To be able to swim unrestricted fin to fin.

Whilst the tang glider enabled you to accept and let go of your relationship with the hook and those related to your fellow fish, you know it is time to say, "Thank you and goodbye."

You will always be grateful to the tang glider because it enabled you to move forward in your life and embrace your potential. But now it is time to find something that will empower you to continue evolving alongside the other fish.

It is time to Carp-pool your resources with those of your fellow fish.

CHAPTER FOURTEEN

CARP-POOLING

"He's a cleaner. She's a director. He's a dentist. She's a postwoman."

How often do you find yourself describing people by the job they do?

We use it in much the same way as we would other descriptors like the colour of someone's hair or their height. I have used people's job titles throughout this book. Before I described their behaviour, had you already formed an opinion of what Paul, Kate, Robert and Richard were like, just from the job they did?

Perhaps your assumptions were correct, or maybe these people surprised you.

We attribute all sorts of meaning to job roles: education, ability, type of person they are, what their reactions might be. We create stories in our heads, which may or may not be true. The fact is, people should never be defined by the job they do.

Like the cleaning supervisor, who had been awarded a medal from his home country in respect of his work with the intelligence service. Or the porter who had been a semi-professional footballer. Or the managing director who was illiterate.

How many times is someone recruited into a role and we then limit our thinking regarding their capabilities? For some reason we believe their abilities only extend as far as the requirements of the job they have been hired for. We conveniently forget about all their other previous experience and skills.

Richard was a football coach, Dave an amazing artist and Kate a national gymnast.

And what about those individuals who join an organisation and have an array of unexploited talents? Very few organisations take the time to uncover them, let alone find ways to use them in their business. Just because an individual leaves school with no qualifications does not mean they have little or no potential to make a difference to our world. Julie is a shining example of this.

And what about those kids who have been part of the gang culture. Determined to make their life count for something, they courageously turn their back on the only world they know. They use their *bad* life experiences for the greater good, often returning to these environments to persuade others they can do the same.

As individuals and organisations we limit ourselves by our thinking. But if we want to create workplaces where people really are treated as their business' greatest asset then we need to shift our mindset. We need to see the potential in everyone and be committed to helping them unleash this to the world. Both for the benefit of themselves and the business.

Carp-pooling allows you and your fellow fish to come together in a way you have never done previously. In the past you would have secretly been fearful of each other because of your unhelpful hooks. Now you have let go of these this is no longer the case. You recognise your own skills and appreciate the abilities of your fellow fish.

And by using your combined skills and working together you will be able to get to the lake so much quicker than if you had chosen to work alone.

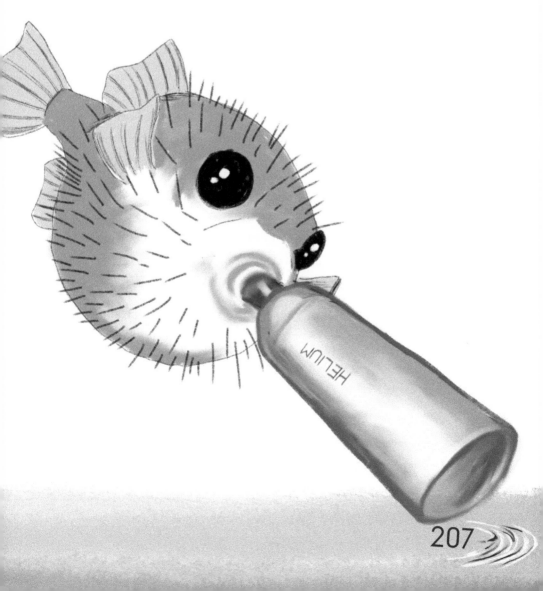

My biggest hero of all is not Freud or any of the other great men and women that have inhabited this planet, but my dad. Not because he's the most intelligent person I have ever met. Or because he left school in Cyprus at thirteen and had to teach himself from then on until he was able to come to university in the UK. But because, without even knowing it, he taught me the importance of treating everyone the same and communicating with them in a way that is meaningful for them.

He is the stereotypical nutty professor. So intelligent, but so lacking in common sense. I can't tell you the number of times he put his glasses in the fridge, left his keys on the outside of the front door or forgot to follow the basic principles of driving on the road because he was too busy thinking about the latest mathematical equation. We called this off-roading.

He also kindly donated untold umbrellas to his fellow travellers who used the Metropolitan Line to travel into central London. If forgetting your umbrella was a divorceable offence, I am sure my mum would have divorced him a hundred times over.

Dad doesn't have a modicum of common sense, but he has a much greater skill. He has the ability to communicate with all people, whether it's the vice chancellor of his university or the plasterer who has come to work on the extension of the house.

Dad always chats about subjects which are important to them and his behaviour never changes no matter who is in the room.

If we adopted this approach at work and stopped judging people by their job role, how different would the workplace be?

There was lots of noise and energy. Looking around the room, people were smiling and laughing. The food—pizza from Domino's—and drink—Sainsbury's own-label beer and wine—was going down well and everyone was enjoying themselves.

A tap of a spoon—cheap Ikea cutlery—on glass—crystal from John Lewis—was meant to bring quiet to the room but had no effect whatsoever—the conversation about the naked man in the ladies loo was too gripping—so someone with a loud voice—me, aka Mel B, hollered, "Ey up! I'll tell you what I want, what I really, really want. For you lot to SHUT UP!"

A few seconds passed and then there was absolute silence.

"I know the past six months has been really tough, but I just wanted to say a massive thank you to each and every one of you," Robert was grinning as he looked round the room at his maintenance team. "We couldn't have got here without you and it's been an entire team effort. And for those of you who may not have heard, for the last couple of weeks we have hit a 75% achievement rate on our SLA targets!"

A massive cheer erupted and when he could finally be heard again, Robert said, "Let's raise a glass to us." As if by magic someone hit *Spice Up Your Life* on their iPod and music filled the room. Stood in the corner, I could not have been happier for Robert and his team.

Six months previously when Robert had decided to change things for himself and his team none of us could have ever known it would lead to this momentous occasion.

For Robert it had been a journey made up of tiny pauses, small moments and big decisions. Change had occurred at all levels. The maintenance team were much happier and more engaged, customer complaints had virtually disappeared and achievement of the SLA targets was at an acceptable level and continuing to rise.

The biggest change of all was in Robert himself. No longer was he running off to find excitement away from campus and his team. He was finding satisfaction in his work home. Already tall at 6 foot 4 inches it felt as though he had grown another foot taller: so proud of all his team had achieved. He was focused on the job in hand and he was loving the success.

It was a wonderful achievement, but the biggest miracle of all came in the form of the team's shift patterns. Having originally taken three years to implement, the working patterns had been revised and realised just six weeks after Robert had thrown down the gauntlet and asked his team for their ideas.

Despite their initial reservations the team had relished the challenge of being involved and it was their suggestions which were finally implemented.

Was it money and profit that had driven these changes? No.

Was it a belief in the power of people to create change? Absolutely.

The knowledge that if you truly believe people are amazing and provide environments and support to help them thrive, they will do just that. And sometimes they will achieve even more than you imagine, completely blowing you away.

Behaviour breeds behaviour.

With the operation running so efficiently, Robert and his team were able to focus on other areas of the business that had previously been neglected—long-term maintenance and service contracts. A further year down the line, the team started making significant savings which meant there was money available to fund wish list projects.

Success breeds success.

If an organisation focuses on its people, the financial rewards will come. But without the grit and heartache of feeling like you are wading through treacle.

Fantastic. Fresh. Fun.

These were the values of the department, when I became director. Previously, when Maleficent had been director, the team had embraced them but always reluctantly because they could sense a disconnect between the behaviours the values demanded and the actions of their director.

The process to identify the values had been thorough and had involved everyone from across the department. They truly reflected the ethos of the entire team and people did not find it difficult to make a connection with their personal values.

When the changes in director occurred there was never any discussion about whether the values should be changed or tweaked. The senior management team and I knew they needed to stay. Whilst there may have been a disconnect with the previous director they were an intrinsic part of the department. They were the driving force for change.

Supporting the vision, the values became part of what we did every day. They underpinned decision-making. And our overall strategy focused on creating a fantastic, fresh and fun environment for everyone in our world. The values helped us kill the tumour that had silently been growing through the department and we were able to break down the silo mentality.

The blame culture transformed into a one team approach where people genuinely supported each other, irrespective of whether it was a good day or one where nothing went right. The 3Fs (as the team shortened them to) became the lifeblood of the department and they provided strong roots from which we could grow and develop.

By carp-pooling with your fellow fish you are able to get to know them in a way you never have before. With your desire for improved communication, you are able to appreciate what motivates and inspires them. You understand their values and how they connect with your own.

And with this comprehension you and your fellow fish are able to make the leap from carp-pooling to the Dirigi-bubble.

The Dirigi-bubble is the final phase of your journey. Fuelled by your shared values it is going to take you and your fellow fish to the place of your dreams, the lake.

The lake, which provides an abundance of clear, free-flowing water, will enable you to fulfil your potential and find true peace and happiness. The journey has been long and arduous, but the final rewards make the struggle and hardship worthwhile.

Of course, not all of your fellow fish will make it to the lake.

Some chose to give up en route, whilst others chose not to embrace the possibilities that change offers and preferred instead to stay where they were. You hope that at some point in the future they may choose to continue their journey, so they too can enjoy all the lake has to offer. But if they don't, you now recognise the decision is theirs alone and there is nothing you can do to influence this.

Find **The Dirigi-bubble** *in your set of scales and complete the following exercise:*

In the *Me* bubble, list all the things that are important to you. They might be your job, your family, your friends. I would have to include my yoga mat because during all those times when my life is crazy my yoga mat represents peace and tranquillity. What else could you not live without?

In the *Organisation* bubble, note everything you believe is important to your business. It might be surplus or profit. It might be

rankings, customer perception or brand. List down everything you can think of.

In the *Values* bubble, write all the values that come to mind. They may be your personal values, your business values, values you think other people may have.

And when you have done this, look at your creation and identify the place where all three bubbles overlap. That place, the place you are looking at, is where the magic and wonder happens in an organisation. It's where an organisation and an individual come together with their shared values and create an environment which is beyond the norm.

An environment where an organisation and its people work in partnership to enjoy individual and team success. Where both parties accept their joint responsibility and accountability for the world they create.

And if you're thinking this is just some bonkers idea or fluffy utopia, it isn't. This approach can and does achieve tangible results. Within just two years of using the 3Fs to drive change, as a department of the University of Studymore, we had increased our bottom-line surplus by 75% from £1.8 million to £3.2 million.

Not only that, but our service which had previously been rated by an external accreditation company as good, achieved the accolade of *World Class*. As a team, we were a finalist in both the leadership category of the British Quality Foundation Excellence Awards and the National Management and Leadership Awards for *Best Management Team*.

Of course, using values to drive business change is challenging. It is not a quick-fix solution, but it is the only way to create sustainable transformation. When done correctly it leaves a lasting legacy.

Three years after I left Studymore, I was busy working at home when a LinkedIn invite popped up on my computer screen. Always eager to know whether it was from someone who actually knew me or some strange interloper from an exotic faraway place like Sydney or Scunthorpe, I clicked on the invitation.

It was from James, who had been a member of the porter team at the University. Fascinated to learn what he had been up to, I dropped him a message asking that very question. Seconds later, I got a response back saying he was still doing the same job, but he wanted to let me know he had just qualified as a coach.

So inspired by the work we had done with FFF, James decided he wanted to learn more about people and their behaviour. Reading his words brought a lump to my throat. 1,095 days, 26,280 hours and

1,576,800 minutes after I had left the University of Studymore our values were still having an impact. That's not change, that's legacy.

A year after that I was at a catering exhibition when I bumped into Studymore's deputy catering manager. There for a chef's competition, Rachel could not wait to show me some of the new initiatives they had introduced which embodied FFF. Once again, not simply change.

Legacy.

As the dirigi-bubble finally helps you land at your lake you have to flutter your fin to make sure you aren't dreaming. The lake is real, no longer a figment of your imagination or part of your vision. It is as beautiful as you knew it would be.

As you swim unrestricted, fin to fin with your fellow fish, you experience complete peace and joy. You can never imagine wanting anything more. Looking up to the sky you realise this isn't in fact a magical lake. It is your Legacy Lake.

It's the gift you will leave the world when you are no longer here.

Just for a moment, fast-forward to the end of your life and consider what it is you want to be remembered for.

Take some time to think about all the different roles you play in your life. Lover, friend, parent, child, manager, work colleague, coach.

And once you have done that, think about how you want these people to remember you. When you are no longer physically here, what do you want people to say about you, how you touched their lives, influenced them and made a difference to their world?

What descriptions would bring up real emotion? That you were a phenomenal manager, a wonderful parent, an inspiring individual.

What would make you laugh?

What would make you cry?

What would make you immensely proud?

You may need to sit with this for a while or just consider one role at a time.

Note down all your thoughts on The Legacy Lake in the set of scales.
Once you have done this find a way to keep it close to you.
After all, it is your gift to mankind.

We will all leave our legacy in this world and right now in this very moment we are creating it. The question is do you want to leave a legacy you have designed or one that has been created by default?

Are you living your life in accordance with your values or just hoping that one day things will change?

Hope is not a strategy and only you have the power to decide how your story ends. Do you want to leave a giant dinosaur-sized imprint on the world or the tiniest of pinpricks?

Will you be the fish that climbs a tree or the one that spends the rest of its life believing it's stupid?

If it's the latter, go back to those people on your scorecard of appreciation and ask them what they think. I bet they think you are completely amazing and can do anything you set your mind to.

And they would be right. Because no matter what you think, the only person holding you back from being totally and utterly brilliant is you.

With the aid of this book you have the opportunity to take steps towards the changes you want to make. To live a life without regrets, one filled with joy and happiness. And whilst it may be a long journey that will require you to be brave and determined, it is an adventure you can complete.

Remember, this is your life, your lifetime, your legacy. Don't be defined by your past or your present. Choose your future. Join the transformation revolution.

Choose to be the fish that climbed a tree.

Mel's Bio

Mel is on a mission.

She wants to create a revolution. A revolution that starts with the belief fish really can climb trees.

Why?

Because everyone one of us is a genius and has the power to be completely and utterly amazing. Sadly, very few people recognise this fact or believe it to be true.

Mel has always had a love of people and when she began her own personal development journey in her late twenties her passion grew even further. She became fascinated by why we choose to do what we do.

Mel has an eclectic mix of qualifications which are reflective of her views about life, "Never limit what you can achieve and always have fun." She is a master practitioner of NLP, has a degree in Hospitality Management, a Masters' in Marketing and has also recently qualified as a creative kinesiologist. Oh, and she's a qualified yoga teacher for children.

Mel has managed large and small teams throughout her career and for the past twenty years much of this work has been at director level. Nothing gives her greater pleasure than seeing people fulfil their potential. In 2015 she set up her own business helping individuals, teams and organisations transform themselves from can't to can.

This book shares her approach and ethos. To find out more go to:

www.fishclimbtrees.co.uk

mel@fishclimbtrees.co.uk

https://www.linkedin.com/in/melanieloizou/

Acknowledgements

Thinking about who I want to thank makes me smile. I may never win an Oscar, but for me, writing this book feels like a similar achievement. And just like all those Oscar winners... there are plenty of people I want to thank.

First and foremost, my gorgeous and amazingly talented daughters, Ellie and Louisa. I learn so much from you every day and you inspire me to be the very best I can. I can't wait for you to unleash your superpowers on this unsuspecting world. It will be a better place for it.

To Jason, who disappeared from my life for a while, only to reappear offering never-ending support, and cups of hot water whilst I was furiously typing away, unable to focus on anything but the words I wanted to write.

To Mum and Dad, who are my greatest advocates. I hope I make you proud.

To Tim. Without whom the world of Fish Climb Trees would never have been created.

And finally, to all my lovely family, friends and clients. This book could not have been written without you. So many of the stories in the book belong to you not me, I'm just grateful I was able to accompany you on the journey.

From the bottom of my heart, thank you.

mPowr Titles

Speak Performance

Ges Ray

ISBN—978-1-907282-87-4

For those afraid of speaking in front of a small team, groups of strangers or large crowds. How to be a confident, compelling and convincing speaker.

Your Slides Suck

David Henson

ISBN—978-1-907282-78-2

For all speakers who need to show information visually. How to make engaging, empowering and effective PowerPoint presentations.

The Key: To Business & Pesonal Success

Martyn Pentecost

ISBN—978-1-907282-17-1

For those who are passionate about growing and developing. How to discover yourself and the most effective ways for you to flourish and enjoy success.

Legacy: You Get One Life... Make It Remarkable

Martyn Pentecost

ISBN—978-1-907282-48-5

For those who truly want to make a difference. How to nurture your legacy through relationships, creativity, family and your work or business.

Storyselling: Your Business

Martyn Pentecost

ISBN—978-1-907282-59-1

For those who wish to go beyond simplistic hero—problem—resolution *approaches to storytelling. How to become a master storyseller by exploring ancient storytelling tradtions and contemporary technological innovations.*

Write Your Book, Grow Your Business

Richard Hagen

ISBN—978-1-907282-54-6

For consultants, trainers, entrepreneurs and busines experts who want to write a book to grow your business. How to avoid the most dangerous pitfalls and set yourself up for maximum succcess before you start to write.

Domestic Abuse Rescue Essentials (DARE)

Diana Onuma

ISBN—978-1-907282-87-92-8

For those facing situations of domestic abuse and those supporting others through these challenges. How to claim your freedom when the need to leave overcomes the reasons to stay.

Mission: Leadership

Ben Morton

ISBN—978-1-907282-71-3

For managers, coaches and leaders. How to create and support strong teams by encouraging heroes, liberating victims and challenging the villains in your workplace.

Lightning Source UK Ltd.
Milton Keynes UK
UKHW041330010419
340279UK00002B/187/P